An Introduction to Keeping Sheep

By
Jane Upton and Dennis Soden

Farming
BOOKS AND VIDEOS

Acknowledgements

Our thanks go to Gill McLellan for her expert typing and practical knowledge of sheepkeeping which assisted in the compilation of the first edition; to Mr A.J. Stevens MA, BVSC, Dip. Bact, MRCVS for his encouragement and advice on some of the diseases affecting sheep; to Hilary Howell who kindly guided us through the maze of legislation affecting the welfare aspects of sheep husbandry; to our families for their continuing forbearance in the way that we have disrupted the domestic scene in our homes; to our friends and also members of the Samall Shepherds' Club. Thank you all !!

First Published in 1991 Farming Press
Second Edition 1996
Reprinted in 2002 by Farming Books and Videos Ltd.
This Softback edition published in 2007

ISBN 978 1 904 871 22 4

A catalogue record for this book is available from the British Library.

Published by
Farming Books and Videos Ltd.
PO Box 536
Preston
PR2 9ZY
www.farmingbooksandvideos.com

Set by Farming Books and Videos Ltd.
Printed and bound in Great Britain by Cromwell Press.

Contents

Colour Plates fall in the centre of the book

Introduction

Those of us who have watched a group of lambs playing in the spring sunshine or seen the miracle of a new-born lamb taking its first breath will readily agree that there is a great deal of pleasure to be experienced in keeping and caring for a flock of sheep.

This book is written from a background of many years of practical experience in large and small flocks of both pedigree and commercial sheep, and it seeks to help and guide those who are keeping sheep for the first time. It describes in detail how and why various practical tasks are carried out and how to avoid some of the pitfalls and awkward situations that can arise from time to time. It describes some of the differences between different types of sheep, and it suggests how, when and where to set about starting a flock.

Chapter One
Getting Started

What has prompted your decision to keep sheep? Are they to act purely as grass mowers with the added bonus of a homegrown, maybe organically produced, supply of meat? Does the prospect of keeping breeding animals appeal? Is there a need to diversify in an existing livestock enterprise?

In any event the sheep will need an area of land on which they can graze. That land will have to be securely fenced, with a supply of water nearby. The prospective owner will have decided whether sufficient spare time is available to care for the sheep throughout the year, and whether help will be available for periods when holidays or sick leave are taken. The amount of time required to give adequate care to the sheep will vary from two short visits per day in the summer after shearing, to frequent visits during each twenty-four hour period during lambing time.

Once these basic requirements have been considered and the decision has been taken to go ahead, it is time to start making plans.

Making Contacts

Sheep keepers come from all walks of life, and there might be a local club where people who keep sheep as a hobby can get together to discuss experiences and organise talks, visits and demonstrations. Your local vet should be able to tell you of others who keep small flocks. Visit local sheep fairs and auction sales and meet and talk with as many sheep keepers as possible.

Assessing the available land

The size of your flock will, to a large extent, be dictated by the amount of land that is available for grazing. Assess the quality and quantity of the herbage growing on it, remembering that you will expect your sheep to live almost entirely from it for up to eight months of the year. Is it 'light' or 'heavy' land? Heavy land is close-textured, usually clay-based and is generally more productive than light land, but it will not stand heavy stocking during periods of high rainfall as it poaches or gets trampled into mud very quickly. Light land is composed of larger particles of soil, is free draining and does not poach so easily, but the herbage growing on it does suffer during periods of hot weather and drought. Remember also when you are assessing the grazing that your flock may increase by as much as two hundred per cent following a very successful lambing.

How many sheep?

Initially stocking rates should be no more than five ewes per hectare. This number can be adjusted in subsequent years if necessary. The sheep will be healthier and more contented if your land is understocked rather than overstocked.

Where to find your sheep

If there is a sheep or shepherd's club operating locally this can be a good source as members often have surplus stock for sale. Look at the small ads in your local paper, or your vet may know of sheep for sale. Be wary of small groups being offered for sale in the local auction market. They may be rejects from a large flock for any number of reasons including the ability to escape from any type of enclosure! However, a trip to a local auction market or sheep fair can be useful as a guide to the value of different classes of sheep and it will give you an idea of how much you must expect to pay when you make your purchase.

If you decide that you would like to keep a pure breed of sheep you will be able to obtain the name and address of the secretary of the breed society from the National Sheep Association, The Sheep Centre, Malvern, Worcestersire WR13 6PH. The secretary will be able to let you know where you can obtain specimens of your preferred breed, and whether any are available in your locality. If one of the rare breeds has taken your fancy, details can be obtained from the Rare Breeds Survival Trust, National Agricultural Centre, Stoneleigh, Warwickshire CV8 2LG.

Chapter Two
What Type of Sheep to Buy

The type of sheep to buy will be determined to a certain extent by what is available and the time of year when you decide to purchase. Most of the sheep fairs and sales of breeding sheep take place between August and November, but sheep from private sources are available at all times of the year. Ewes of four or five years of age that have already produced lambs are probably the best buy for beginners as they will be experienced in motherhood. Another possibility is to buy weaned ewe lambs in the autumn but not to mate them until the autumn of the following year. This will give the beginner an opportunity to get to know the sheep and how to handle them. Ewe lambs are much lighter in weight and the various tasks are more easily carried out with them than with heavier sheep. You will become more proficient in handling as their weight increases!

If the sheep are required purely to keep grass under control, then consider buying wether lambs, i.e. castrated males, as their feed requirements are less than for breeding ewes. They are usually sold by their breeders in the autumn and fattened during the next few months before being sold for meat. If they are kept as grass mowers then they will need to be shorn and dipped in the spring, and will have increased considerably in size and weight by the following autumn. They can then be sold for meat and replacement lambs purchased. The main drawback to this is that they will be offered for sale at a time when smaller, younger lambs are also being sold for meat, and the price per kilo tends to decrease as the weight and age of the sheep increase. Yet another possibility is to buy wether lambs of a longwoolled or finewoolled breed and keep them for a number of years, using the income from their high-value fleeces as a contribution towards the cost of keeping them.

Conformation

There are certain basic standards which should be looked for:

The sheep should have a good mouth with incisor teeth which meet the pad on the top jaw in the correct position

– neither overshot nor undershot.

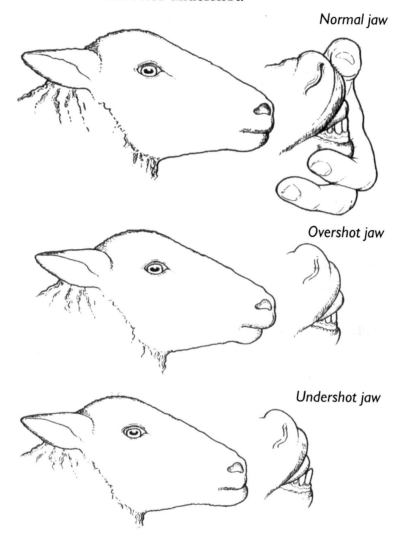

Normal jaw

Overshot jaw

Undershot jaw

There should be good strong bone and straight legs, not bowing inwards or outwards. Pay particular attention to the hind legs of rams. Ensure that there are no weaknesses in the pastern, which is the joint immediately above the foot. Any weakness there can affect the performance

Good overall conformation

Strong bone and
Straight Legs

A weak pastern   A good foot

Legs should not be bowing
outwards or inwards

of rams and ewes kept for breeding.

A long level back is desirable with a good spring of rib giving plenty of room for the heart and lungs.

Which Breed to Buy

There are over eighty different breeds of sheep in the United Kingdom, including recent imports from overseas, all trying to find a niche in the British sheep industry. The British breeds can be categorised into three main types; Shortwools, Longwools and Hill or Mountain.

The Shortwools

These include the Down breeds which were developed in the southern half of England by using a Southdown ram on ewes of various local breeds.

The Southdown was fixed as a breed and generally improved for meat production by selection from within the breed by John Ellman at Glynde near Lewes in Sussex during the 18th century. At the beginning of the 20th century huge flocks, by today's standards at least, were kept on large estates, producing lamb and mutton of the first quality. By the end of the Second World War numbers had fallen dramatically as meat rationing and the general food shortage gave quantity precedence over quality, and the breed has never recovered its former popularity.

Another reason for the decline of the breed was the shortage of shepherds willing or qualified to work with such labour-intensive flocks. In recent years Southdowns have been imported from New Zealand in an attempt to make the breed more acceptable to modern conditions. They are longer-bodied and longer in the leg than their original UK forebears, without losing the quality for which the breed is famed.

The Southdown was used to develop the other Down breeds by crossing with local breeds to produce the Hampshire Down, the Dorset Down, the Suffolk and the Oxford Down in various parts of the country.

Because of their docility and close flocking instinct, Down breeds were used to improve the fertility of the soil through a system known as folding. The sheep were confined by a temporary fence of hurdles or wire netting to a small area of a crop grown specially for them. Each day they were moved on to a fresh area so that their dung was distributed evenly over the field. This benefited subsequent grain crops and at the time was one of the principal sources of fertility, especially on outlying areas of the farm.

The Down breeds are now almost entirely used to produce terminal sires for crossing with the Masham, Mule, Scottish and Welsh Halfbreds and similar crossbred ewes where the progeny are destined for the meat market.

The Hampshire Down
The origin of this breed stems from crosses between the Southdown and the Wiltshire Horn and the now extinct Berkshire Knot. Centred on Hampshire, Wiltshire and Berkshire, it is a breed which at the present time is used

mainly as a terminal sire of very early-maturing butcher's lambs. Many pedigree flocks are Meat and Livestock Commission recorded and have their lambs' backfat scanned and so breed from lean, fast-growing sheep.

The Dorset Down

This medium sized, brownfaced breed evolved in the parish of Wool, in Dorset, in the 1820s, and is the result of using a Southdown ram on Hampshire and Wiltshire ewes. Dorset ewes will take the ram at most times of the year. The lambs are very early maturing, whether from purebred stock or from crossbred ewes, and regularly give a carcase of 18kg in 12 weeks. The wool quality is among the highest of the native British breeds and considerable quantities go to the hosiery trade.

The Oxford Down

One of the main attributes of the breed is its ability to sire lambs which have the potential to grow to heavy weights without excess fat. The carcases are ideal for boning and rolling as they are large with a good depth of lean meat. Mature rams of this breed can weigh over 150kg.

The Suffolk

This is the main terminal breed sire in the UK being used in 70 percent of prime lamb-producing crossbred flocks. It has a distinctive clean black head and legs and was first recognised as a pure breed in 1810. It evolved from crossing Southdown rams with Norfolk Horn ewes which ran on the heathlands of East Anglia. There are over 2000 pedigree Suffolk breeders in the UK, distributed all over the country, and ram sales are held countrywide. Suffolk cross lambs are early maturing, reaching slaughter weight in 12 to 14 weeks; they can grow on to heavier weights later in the year without producing excess fat. Many producers use the Suffolk sired crossbred ewe lambs as commercial dams in their flocks, producing prime lambs, particularly the Suffolk X Scotch Halfbred and the Suffolk X Mule and Masham.

The Shropshire

Following the establishment of the breed in the 19th century, the Shropshire reached its peak of popularity early in the 20th. It went into decline in the 1920s and it was not until the 1980s that it began to make a recovery. Today it is a sheep well-suited to present-day requirements, whether it is bred pure or used as a crossing sire.

The Dorset Horn

Both the Dorset Horn and its sister breed the Polled Dorset, which was developed in Australia, share an important characteristic in that they will breed at almost any time of the year. In some cases it is possible to breed three crops of lambs in two years. The ewes are exceptionally good milkers which explains why their progeny can make high-quality carcases at ten weeks of age.

The Ryeland

The Ryeland is a whitefaced breed rather similar in appearance to the Southdown. It is a breed of great antiquity and its origins in the county of Hereford go back 800 years. Its wool is of high quality and as a breed it is very docile.

The Clun Forest

The Clun Forest is another breed which has declined in popularity since the years just after the Second World War, when it was in great demand. It originates from south-west Shropshire adjoining the Welsh Border and it is a very adaptable breed, being found in most parts of the UK. The ewe is a prolific breeder and produces excellent prime lambs when crossed with Down breed sires. When mated to the Border Leicester she produces the increasingly popular English Halfbred, which is in demand as a commercial ewe.

The Kerry Hill

This black and white, strikingly handsome breed from the Kerry Hills of Montgomeryshire probably had a common origin with the Welsh Mountain sheep and was recognised as a distinct breed before the beginning of the 19th century. Although not numerically strong, it is particularly suited to ley farming. The Kerry Hill ewe is prolific and a good milker, producing good-quality prime lambs when crossed with Down breed rams.

There are several breeds from Wales and the Welsh

borders which represent the transition from the breeds of the mountains to those found on the lower altitude of the uplands and into the lowlands. These include the Hill Radnor, the Beulah and the Lleyn.

The Hill Radnor

The Hill Radnor is equally at home on the hills, uplands and lowlands of the Welsh Marches, where it was developed many years ago. It was bred pure with the ewe lambs for replacements on the hills and the wether lambs either sold for meat straight off their dams or sold to lowland farmers for further fattening. It has a tan face and legs and is extremely hardy, docile and under favourable conditions it is a prolific breeder with adequate milk for its lambs.

The Beulah Speckled Face

This breed is bigger and less hardy than true mountain sheep and because of a management system where they spend part of the year confined in fields they are much more docile. It is a very handsome breed with a black and white face and a fleece of clean, soft, white wool. As a pure breed the ewes can produce butcher's lambs of 36kg liveweight in 12 to 15 weeks. In recent years the Border Leicester and the Bluefaced Leicester rams have been used to provide Welsh Mule ewe lambs for commercial flocks.

The Lleyn

Lleyn sheep take their name from the Lleyn peninsula

in North Wales. They are medium-sized, polled and whitefaced. Although their numbers declined in post-war years, they were rescued by a few devotees of the breed and are now firmly established again. High prolificacy, strong mothering instinct and high milk yield enable it to produce prime carcases of around 20kg from grass.

The Longwools

Generally speaking, the Longwools are larger sheep which mature more slowly than the Shortwools. They were more popular when families were larger and consequently larger joints of mutton were required. Their fleeces provided an income from the relatively poorer hill areas of the Cotswolds and the Yorkshire and Lincolnshire Wolds. These areas are the homes of the Cotswold, the Leicester and the Lincolnshire Longwool breeds. The Longwool group also includes the Romney Marsh, which originates from the low-lying area of that name in Kent.

The Romney

These sheep have the ability to withstand very high stocking densities and can carry a higher worm burden than other breeds without showing ill-effect. It has been exported successfully to many parts of the world and on to all kinds of terrain. When crossed with the Southdown ram in New Zealand, it was responsible from the famous Canterbury lamb. The Romney is still the most popular breed in the area which bears its name.

Some of the Longwools, notably the border Leicester, the Teeswater, the Wensleydale and the Hexham or Bluefaced Leicester, are used almost exclusively to produce rams for crossing with ewes of the hill breeds. The resulting ewe lambs from this cross are sold to lowland farmers, either as lambs or as 18 month old ewes, where they are mated with Shortwool rams to produce prime lamb for the meat market.

The Teeswater

The Teeswater is from the Northern Pennines where, for at least 150 years, it has been bred by farmers to provide rams for crossing with Hill ewes, mostly Swaledale, Dalesbred, Rough Fell and Herdwick. The resulting cross is known as the Masham – a highly prolific sheep much in demand by commercial prime lamb producers. The Teeswater is a medium-sized, hornless breed with a long, lustrous fleece. It has been developed over the years on purely commercial lines and it is judged by the qualities of its Masham progeny. Fancy points are largely ignored and the ram is rarely used for pure breeding until it has proved itself as a breeder of good-quality Mashams. The Masham wether lamb can, under a variety of conditions, produce a long, lean, prime carcase ideally suited to today's needs. The Teeswater is an exceptionally prolific, heavy-milking ewe, and lambing averages of 250 to 300 percent are not uncommon.

The Border Leicester

This breed was established in Scotland some 250 years

ago, and results from crosses between the Cheviot and English Leicester breeds. It is a large, white-faced and hornless breed, and is used principally to produce high-quality female progeny when crossed with the smaller Hill breeds. When crossed with the Cheviot the progeny are known as the Scottish halfbred, with the Blackface it is known as the Scottish Greyface, and with the Welsh Mountain it produces the Welsh Halfbred. All of these crossbred ewes are used by commercial farmers to breed prime-quality lamb when put to terminal sires of the Down breeds.

The Hexham or Bluefaced Leicester

The importance of this breed lies in the qualities it imparts to its crossbred offspring. It is a large sheep and the rams are used chiefly on the Swaledale, Dalesbred, Rough Fell and Herdwick ewes, the lambs being known as the North of England Mule.

Further descriptions of the qualities attributed to the Mule and Masham crossbred ewes are to be found on pages 28 and 29 under the Swaledale and Dalesbred headings.

The Wensleydale

This is a large, bluefaced sheep with a long, lustrous fleece. Both ewes and rams will produce up to 7kg of wool with a staple length of 30cm. Its main use is for crossing with the Hill breeds to produce commercial ewes which are prolific and heavy-milking and which, when mated with terminal sires, are producers of prime-quality lambs.

Other members of this group include the Dartmoor, the Devon and Cornwall Longwool and the Devon Closewool, which come from the high rainfall areas of south-west England. Mature rams of the Devon and Cornwall breed can produce around 16kg of wool annually, as can rams of the Lincoln, Leicester and Cotswold breeds.

The Devon Closewool

North Devon, where the breed originated and from which it has spread over large areas of south-west England, is one of the most densely sheep-populated areas of the world. Rarely seen outside the south-west, the Devon Closewool is medium-sized with a white face and produces a good fleece of 3 to 4kg of medium-quality wool used for hosiery and tweeds. Many flocks live entirely off grass all the year round.

The Dartmoor

The Greyfaced Dartmoor is a sheep whose fleece and constitution have been developed to cope with the extreme climatic conditions of the bleak moorland which is its home. Numerically it is not as strong as many other breeds. The wool is long in staple and lustrous, and fleeces from yearling rams average 12kg in weight with an individual fibre length of 22cm. The Whitefaced Dartmoor, another breed found on the moor, has, as its name implies, a white face. It is very hardy, being kept out on the moor from May to December. Formerly all of the breeds were horned but now the majority, particularly of the ewes, are polled.

The Cotswold

The Cotswold is a large whitefaced sheep of great antiquity. A Cotswold shearling ram will produce a fleece of up to 12kg in weight, while fleeces from shearling ewes range from 5.5 to 6.75kg. In the Middle Ages Cotswold sheep were the chief source of the wealth which enabled wool merchants to build many of the attractive stone manor houses and churches seen in the Cotswold Hills today. The breed was used in the early 19th century to cross with Hampshire Down ewes to produce the Oxford Down.

In the 1960s the breed became almost extinct, the total ewe flock being confined to just one owner. From the dispersal of this flock, a number of small flocks were started and since then numbers have grown. A flock book has been started and the future of this famous breed is now assured.

The Hill Breeds

The hill breeds occupy a unique position in the sheep industry in that their distribution covers a huge area of high land which is largely unsuitable for any other type of farming. Two qualities which all the hill breeds possess are hardiness and thriftiness. Hardiness gives them the ability to withstand severe climatic conditions, and thriftiness the ability to thrive on a limited food supply, often of poor quality.

They are smaller sheep than either of the two previous categories and, unlike the Down breeds, they have evolved a habit of scattered grazing. They spread themselves thinly on the ground so that there is less competition for the available grazing. When enclosed in a lowland situation they regard a field boundary as a challenge to see what lies beyond, as they believe the grass is always greener on the other side. This behaviour is understandable when it is appreciated that they are the descendants of animals which have been given free range over a huge area of countryside for many hundreds of years.

The Blackface

The Blackface is numerous in Scotland, Ireland, the north of England and the moors of south-west England. It is a hardy, horned breed with a fleece that helps it to withstand the heavy rainfall, high winds and harsh winters of these areas. There are several different types within the breed which have evolved to match the environmental conditions. The Perth type is large-framed with a medium to heavy fleece and is found mainly in north-east Scotland, south-west England and Ireland. The Northumberland has a softer fleece and is used to produce the North of England Mule when mated with the Hexham Leicester. The Lanark type, which has combined with the Newton

Stewart and covers much of Scotland and Ireland, has a shorter fleece and an improved milking ability over other types of Blackface.

The breed is bred pure for four or five years to provide flock replacements, and they are then sold on to kinder land and mated with either the Border Leicester to produce Greyface ewe lambs, or the Hexham or Bluefaced Leicester. Both crosses provide prolificacy and good mothering qualities for the production of prime butcher's lambs when mated to terminal sires.

Blackface rams intended for shows and sales are sometimes dipped in a solution containing an orange/ yellow dye in an attempt to enhance their appearance. This is called bloom dipping and can be seen on the ram illustrated. Bloom dipped fleeces purchased by the British Wool Marketing Board attract a penalty.

The Swaledale

The Swaledale is probably the strongest breed of sheep numerically, and it is found mainly in the north of England. It is a very hardy breed with a distinctly marked face – the upper part dark and the lower part white or mealy. It has a fleece which is softer than could reasonably be expected from a hardy hill breed. Except at the back of the head, where it is mixed with black, the wool is white with a thick, deep bed and curly top. The Swaledale ewes, which are bred pure initially, are sold at around five years of age and crossed with Teeswater or

Bluefaced Leicester rams for the production of much sought-after ewe lambs. The cross from the Teeswater is known as the Masham, and from the Blueface Leicester the North of England Mule. These crosses are to be found in all areas of the UK, where prolificacy, excellent mothering qualities and the heavy milk yields combine with the early maturity from the Down breed sires to give top-quality butcher's lambs.

The Dalesbred

As its name implies, the Dalesbred, which is a cousin of the Swaledale, was developed in the Western Dales of Yorkshire and adjoining areas. It was fixed as a distinct breed in 1930. It has a dark face, a mealy nose and a white mark on each side of its nostrils. Its wool is softer than the Swaledale's, with a dense undercoat and a curly top with no black fibres. As a breed it is used to graze the high ground and to produce three or four crops of purebred ewes, after which the ewes are sold to go to lower ground where they are crossed with the Teeswater and Hexham Leicester rams to provide prolific, milky female progeny, which are again sold on as the dams of prime lambs when crossed with Down breeds.

The Rough Fell

This is a hardy, long-lived breed which is well fitted to endure the rigours of the high mountains and valleys of the Lake District and the Yorkshire Dales. Both sexes are horned and have a long, coarse fleece which is used for carpets and mattresses. The ewes breed purebred lambs for three or four crops before being sold to farms on kinder land for a further three or four crops of crossbred lambs, the females from which go on to be the dams of prime lambs.

The Herdwick

The Herdwick holds pride of place for hardiness and can exist on the sparse and poor-quality grazing of the Lake District and High Fells under wintry conditions, often without any supplementary feeding. It is a white-faced breed and only the rams have horns. The lambs are born with black fleeces but as mature sheep the wool fades to a blue-grey colour. The ewes are allowed to mature before being mated, and shearling ewes are not always put to the ram. A mature ewe weighs from 35 to 45kg, and under hill conditions will produce a 90 percent lamb crop. When taken from the fells and put onto a reasonable plane of nutrition, they are more prolific and will produce a good butcher's lamb to a terminal sire.

The Lonk

The Lonk is one of the largest of the native hill breeds. It hails from the Lancashire and Yorkshire Pennines, and can be traced back to 1740. The face is black and white and both sexes are horned. The fleece is of a higher quality than is normally carried by hill breeds. The wool is white and free of kemp. Lonk rams are occasionally used to introduce prolificacy and size into other hill breeds without sacrificing the hardiness for which they are renowned.

The Exmoor Horn

The Exmoor Horn is a hill breed which does equally well on moorland grazing. It is whitefaced with horns, and carries a white fleece of medium length and good quality. The draft ewes are in demand for crossing with the Bluefaced Leicester to produce the Exmoor Mule for lowland areas.

The Derbyshire Gritstone

A black-and whitefaced hill sheep from the Peak District of Derbyshire, the breed is polled in both sexes. The Gritstone is hardy and thrifty and many flocks spend their entire lives on the hills. When bred pure it is capable of producing prime finished lamb off unimproved land up to 2000 feet above sea level. It crosses well onto the other hill breeds, improving size, carcase quality and wool.

The Cheviot

A whitefaced sheep of the Scottish Borders. When bred pure it can produce a quality lamb of 17kg but more usually the wether lambs are overwintered and fed on turnips on lower land to reach a carcase weight of around 21kg. The draft ewes from the hill were originally crossed with the Border Leicester to produce the famous Scottish Halfbred. Now the Bluefaced Leicester is also used to produce the Cheviot Mule, the females from both crosses making excellent mothers of quality lamb for the meat market. Cheviot rams have been used in Wales on the Welsh Moutain ewe to produce the Brecknock Cheviot which is now fixed as a separate breed.

The North Country Cheviot

This breed originated as the Cheviot in the border country between England and Scotland. In the 18th century a large number were driven north to occupy land depopulated by the Highland Clearances. Occasional crossing of the Cheviot with the Leicester breed led to a larger-bodied sheep, which is now firmly established and can be seen in large numbers in the most northerly counties of Scotland.

The Welsh Mountain

The Welsh Mountain comes in a number of different types. It varies between the small, extremely hardy sheep of the high mountains to the larger type of the common land around the valleys of South Wales. All have white or tan faces and are extremely thrifty, being active foragers. After a spell of pure breeding, the draft ewe crosses well with the Border Leicester and the Bluefaced Leicester, producing the Welsh Halfbred and the Welsh Mule. Many Welsh ewes are bred to Down rams, and the mothering qualities and the milking ability of the ewe are such that comparatively young lambs grow to a size greater than their dams. Welsh Mountain lamb and mutton is lean, tender and unsurpassed for flavour and comes in the small joints which are popular today, the carcases finishing at from 11 to 18kg.

One feature of the Welsh Mountain is that it is a very active sheep and as such is difficult to confine, especially when brought onto low ground. Any kind of fence will be closely inspected and if at all possible an escape route through, under or over will be found. This is understandable when one realises that in the high mountains the sheep's very survival depended on its being able to seek out meagre grazing ahead of its flock mates. In consequence, as a breed, it was necessary to spread itself thinly over the ground.

There are a number of variations of the Welsh Moutain. Some are the result of a recessive gene occurring in the traditional flock. The Black Welsh Mountain with its all-black face and wool; the Torddu or Badgerfaced with black eye stripes and black belly; and the Torwen which has the reverse colouring, white belly and white face markings on a dark coloured body – all have similar characteristics to their white ancestors. They lamb easily, are hardy and thrifty and are attractive in appearance.

There are some other British breeds which do not fit neatly into any of the three main categories discussed. These include the Wiltshire Horn, the Jacob and the Shetland.

The Wiltshire Horn

Unique among British breeds of sheep, the Wiltshire Horn does not carry any wool. It is a lowland breed, an excellent converter of grass, and the breed and its crosses can reach carcase weights of 20kg off grass with little or no concentrates. There are no shearing costs and fly and tick problems are virtually unknown. It is an excellent prime lamb sire, and the rams are extremely active and prepotent in that they transmit liveliness to their lambs at birth and achieve early maturity. The ewes are very protective mothers and the absence of wool means that the newborn lamb can find the teats easily. At birth the lamb has a covering of fine hair which protects it from the cold, and the fine, narrow head and neck make for easy lambing.

The Jacob

The Jacob is a very popular sheep with small flock owners as it is a prolific, commercially viable breed which is instantly recognisable by its black and white patterned fleece. It comes in polled, two-horned and multi-horned varieties and its devotees claim a high resistance to foot problems. The high quality wool in two distinct colours enables interestingly patterned garments to be made from natural, undyed yarns. It meets a ready demand from home spinners.

The Shetland

The Shetland is one of the smallest breeds of British Sheep. It is noted for the fineness and softness of its wool and the flavour of its meat. Only the rams are horned and the fleeces come in several shades of colours – white, grey, moorit (reddish brown), fawn and brown.

Recently an attempt has been made to produce a fine-woolled sheep for the hills which will give a heavier fleece and a ewe which will give a prime lamb without the necessity for crossing. The new breed is called the Lomond and comes from crosses between the Shetland and the English Merino.

Rare Breeds

These are mainly British breeds that have lost their popularity over the years for various reasons, as fashions come and go in the sheep world and as the demand for meat and wool changes. Many breeds which were popular earlier this century faced extinction after the Second World War. Many traditional breeds were developed by farmers to meet the particular requirement of a small local area, but with a wider dissemination of knowledge and an efficient transport system, sheep could be taken far from their home base to perform as well as, if not better than, they did at home. These rare breeds are now being saved from extinction mainly by interested hobby farmers and rare breed establishments.

In order to rescue some of the breeds and to preserve their genes for possible future use, the Rare Breeds Survival Trust was formed. The contributions received from members maintain registration facilities for all the breeds which do not have breed societies. The Trust also keeps a directory and can put prospective members in touch with owners of the breed selected.

The rare breeds include a number of multi-horned breeds – the black Hebridean and the brown Manx Loghtan. The

North Ronaldsay from the Orkney Islands has adapted its diet so that it can live on seaweed, and the Boreray exists mostly as a feral flock on the island of that name in the St.Kilda group.

The Portland

The Portland is an attractive, small, tan-faced sheep, originating in south-west England. Together with the Merino it is believed to be an ancestor of today's Dorset Horn. As a breed it is not prolific, very few of the ewes producing twins, but it does produce a lean, lightweight carcase of great flavour.

The Llanwenog

The Llanwenog was fixed as a distinct breed in the relative isolation of the Teifi valley in the late 19th century. Imported Shropshire rams were used on a local horned, bluefaced sheep and it has now developed into a dark-faced grassland sheep producing prime meat lambs. It is very prolific, and lambing percentages of over 200 percent have been recorded by the Meat & Livestock Commission. It crosses well with all the terminal sires and also with the traditional sires of crossbred ewes retained for commercial prime lamb production.

The Soay

The Soay bears a close resemblance to the wild mouflon sheep and all the present Soay stock is descended from the flock on the island of Soay in the St. Kilda group. It is a brownfaced sheep with either fawn or chocolate coloured wool. Mature ewes weigh around 25kg. Lambing difficulties are rare, and the lambs are very active as soon as they are born. Both sexes are horned.

The Norfolk Horn

This breed was rescued from the brink of extinction in the mid 1950s and, thanks to a grading-up programme using Suffolks, is now once again firmly established. It is a heathland sheep from East Anglia, blackfaced, with both sexes horned. Its cross with the Southdown in the early 18th century produced the modern Suffolk.

Breeds from Abroad

In recent years many breeds have been imported into the UK from various parts of the world.

The Texel

One of the earliest imports was the Texel, brought in from Holland and France. It was imported to improve the conformation and carcase quality of the native breeds, particularly leanness and in the leg of mutton (gigot). The Texel figures prominently among the prizewinners of carcase competitions, whether purebred or crossed.

The Charollais

This is another breed making a name for itself as a very good carcase sheep. It comes from France and is a medium-sized, heavy sheep. It ranks highly among terminal sires through the identification of superior genetic material within the breed, and the best are used extensively in leading flocks.

The Bleu du Maine
Also from France comes the Bleu du Maine, a large breed with a slate blue face and legs. It has made headway not just as a terminal sire where its progeny can be taken to all weights without getting too fat, but also as the sire of crossbred ewes from upland flocks, giving improved conformation and proflicacy in their offspring.

The Rouge de l'Ouest
Another terminal sire from France which has performed consistently well in performance testing trials at Loughgall in Northern Ireland. It is a breed which is fertile all the year round and it can also pass this fertility on to its crossbred progeny, an important factor of those who wish to provide out-of-season lamb without recourse to scientific interference.

The Vendeen, Cotentin and Berrichon du Cher
These breeds, all from France, expect to give increased returns through their crossbred progeny by improving carcase quality.

The Est à Laine Merino
This is a large whitefaced breed which breeds naturally all the year round without the use of hormone implants and injections. Its Merino ancestry means that it carries a fleece of very fine wool, a characteristic which is passed

on to its crossbred progeny, giving greatly increased returns from the sale of fleeces off the ewes kept in commercial flocks.

The Polwarth

The main claim to fame of this breed is in the quality of its wool. It is slower maturing but this enables a wool clip to be taken before the lambs are sold, and it has a lean carcase at slaughter. The Polwarth originates from Australia and has been imported into this country from Tasmania. The very fine wool, which comes from its Merino ancestry, is used in the production of high quality worsted cloths. Mature ewes will shear 6 to 7kg of wool and lambs 3 to 4kg at six months. Recently this wool has been making £3 per kg.

The Merino

The Merino originated in Spain. In spite of a monopoly imposed by the Spanish king, specimens of the breed were smuggled into other parts of Europe in the 18th century. Its fine wool was a unique and profitable crop, so although it had no pretensions as a meat breed, it spread rapidly throughout Europe.

By early in the 19th century the Merino had arrived in Australia, and the era of fine wool production in the southern hemisphere had begun. Since then the breed has been developed and used in the formation of many different breeds in practically all parts of the world. Today a Merino ram produces around 10kg of wool annually and a ewe 8kg.

New Zealand Southdown

See the Southdown breed description earlier in this chapter.

These must appear as a bewildering number of breeds for the beginner who is trying to decide which to keep. In making a decision there are a number of factors which need to be considered. Some breeds are more docile than others, and some are endowed with a wanderlust which makes them difficult to enclose in small fields. Body size and weight vary enormously, and this fact should be borne in mind by those who might have difficulty in handling the sheep. Home spinners may be attracted by a particular wool quality or colour, whilst others might go for the visual attraction of horns, face colour or markings.

There is a breed to satisfy just about every requirement!

Chapter Three
Planning your Sheep Area

Fencing

Before purchasing your sheep, make sure that the enclosure is securely fenced. If the sheep are allowed to escape they can be a constant source of annoyance to yourself and to your neighbours. The fence can be a natural hedge but unless it is one that has recently been laid the sheep will browse on it and eventually create weak spots. Avoid poisonous species such as yew, rhododendron etc. to which they might be attracted at certain times of the year, particularly when grass is in short supply. Brambles can become entangled in the wool so that the sheep is unable to free itself, and the bark can be stripped from hedgerow and cultivated species in the spring when the sap is rising, thus ring-barking and killing trees and bushes.

Far superior is well-erected fence consisting of a stock fence with a code number of C8/80/15. This is of rectangular mesh wire, with the mesh graduated so that the smallest mesh is near the ground so as to prevent the sheep putting their heads through and either getting stuck or exerting undue pressure so as to weaken the fence. Avoid using any stock fencing with a larger mesh size than C8/80/15.

This netting is 800mm high and additional height can be obtained by adding strands of plain or barbed wire above it. A strand of barbed wire below the fence at ground level will prevent stock from creeping underneath and will also discourage dogs and predators coming in from the opposite direction.

Any wire fence is only as sound as its construction, and it is vitally important that the fence is correctly tensioned and the supporting stakes are not more than two metres apart. The strainer posts at either end of a straight run of fencing should be at least 900mm into the ground, tightly rammed and well strutted. Somewhere on the fence, either at a strainer post or anywhere along its length, fit a means of tightening the wire when it becomes slack through age or frequent atmospheric temperature changes. Eye bolts, winders and radisseurs can be used as tensioners. When erecting the fence do not drive the holding staples into the intermediate stakes beyond the point where they just touch the wire. This will allow the wire to move through the staples when tensioning or when expansion or contraction occurs. The staples should be at a slight angle when driven into the stakes so that they enter different grains in the wood and avoid splitting.

If the fence is to reinforce a hedge, it should be sited a few feet away from the hedge. This keeps the sheep from climbing onto the fence to feed on the growing tips of the hedge plants and subsequently weakening it. Such behaviour can be discouraged by fitting a single line of electric fence wire so that it projects at right angles from the intermediate fence posts about 150mm from the top of the wire netting.

Electric fencing can be used as an alternative to the stock fencing. It can be in the form of netting or single

Strainer post with strut

line wires. The netting consists of nylon mesh with fine lightweight wire twisted into it to carry the electric current. Single strands of the same materials are also available for use with insulators on wooden posts or on metal posts with built-in insulators. More permanent electric fences using No. 12 galvanised steel wire with insulators on metal or wooden posts does not

A Radisseur

suffer damage from rabbits and hares as the nylon netting sometimes does. The number of line wires (two or three) and the distance between the wires and the total height of the fence will vary according to the breed.

It is advisable to use an electric fence unit connected via a transformer to the mains electricity supply, or if a portable source of electricity is required use a battery operated fencer unit. Batteries have a habit of running down at critical times, weekends, holidays, etc. The best way to make sure a battery does not run out is to have two, one in the field and the other at home being topped up by a trickle charger. Care should be taken at all times to prevent the electric fencing from becoming ineffective through earthing by allowing

Staples in correct position for free movement of the wire

herbage to grow on to it, or by allowing it to come into contact with metal which is not insulated. Very young lambs do not respect electric fencing in the same way

43

as adult sheep. As their small hooves make very light contract with the ground they receive no shock from the fence, and they can become entangled in the electrified netting. However, electric fencing is a good option when the grazing is rented rather than owned, as it can be taken away if use of the land is lost, and put up somewhere else at no further expense. Portable electric fencing is also very useful for making temporary divisions in a field.

If possible site any gate in the boundary fence near a corner of the grazing area. This will make it easier when moving the sheep. It will also be an advantage if the gate opens through 180 degrees: some of the sheep, especially young lambs, will inevitably go to the wrong side if it is at 90 degrees. If the entrance to the grazing is to be used frequently it is advisable to raise the level of the gateway a few inches above the surrounding land with hard core or scalpings so that it remains free from mud even in the worst weather conditions.

Housing

The grass on the grazing area makes little or no growth through the winter months and both sheep and land will benefit from being rested. During this time the sheep will need supplementary feed and it makes it more comfortable for sheep and shepherd if the flock can be kept under cover for a few weeks. This is also a convenient way of buying extra acres if the food consumed at this time has been grown elsewhere.

The sheep house need not be an elaborate building, and it is sufficient to use a simple pole barn construction. Posts which have been pressure-treated with preservative e.g. secondhand telegraph poles, will last much longer in the ground than untreated ones. A mono-pitch roof will be sufficient and the building should be sited with its back to the prevailing wind with a good overhang to the roof both front and back. If the front overhang is angled downwards, it will prevent rain from blowing onto the bedding.

Barley straw provides the best bedding material. It is superior to wheat, rye or oat straw, all of which very soon get trampled flat whereas barley straw stays light and open textured for much longer. The straw should be clean, bright and free from mould. The ewes will pick it over, eating most of the 'flag' or leaf from the stems. Soiled bedding should be cleared from the house periodically to prevent the build-up of moist heat which can lead to foot problems.

Allow four square metres for each ewe. This will also allow you to accommodate the lambs if necessary. The building should have solid walls to the back and ends to a height of 1200mm, with Yorkshire cladding, consisting of narrow vertical boards with a 20mm gap between them, above. Heavyweight perforated plastic can also be used but this is difficult to tension. Such construction will allow adequate ventilation with no draught at floor level.

A sheep house

The fence at the front can be combined with a feed barrier which will enable the sheep to be fed without entering the pen. There must be sufficient space for all the sheep including shy feeders to feed comfortably. A minimum width of 500mm per animal is recommended. The entrance to the house should be a gate not less than 2m in width. The ideal floor is made from rammed chalk, but hardcore covered with smaller material will also be satisfactory. The height of the finished floor should be above the level of the surrounding land so as to avoid problems with drainage. Solid concrete floors should be avoided as the bedding quickly becomes damp and respiratory problems can arise. You may prefer to feed your sheep on a hardstanding in front of the building. Again, the feed can be placed in the troughs without interference from the sheep and you will be able to inspect them more easily.

Water should be available at all times in small valve-operated troughs with provision made for any water resulting from leakages or blocked valves being directed outside the building. If there is a supply of water available from a conventional cattle drinking trough, provide a step or build up the surrounding area so that the sheep can drink comfortably. When young lambs are present, float a heavy plank of wood on the surface of the water. This will carry the weight of any lamb jumping onto the trough when playing and save it from drowning. It will also prevent the growth of algae in the trough during warm weather.

Handling Pens

When the building is no longer required for holding sheep, it can also be used as a handling pen. First clear all the soiled litter from the floor and give a liberal dressing of lime. For small numbers of sheep the only other equipment needed is two or three hurdles hinged together with string and fixed at one end to a side wall of the house. These can be opened out straight and then closed around the sheep, holding them in a confined space while dosing, vaccinating, etc.

If no housing is available then a small, securely fenced enclosure should be constructed in a corner of the field, preferably near the entrance or exit gate. It should consist of a pen large enough to hold all your sheep together, with a small area for individual handling. It is also advisable to build a funnel approach to the pen as this will make penning so much easier. A piece of hessian or similar material stretched between two people can be useful when driving sheep into a narrowing entrance to the pen. If it is found necessary to have a hard floor to the outdoor handling pen, this can be made from loose pebbles around 25mm to 50mm in diameter. These will revolve as the sheep walk on them and are self-cleaning. A retaining board around the outside of the pen will be required to prevent the pebbles from spreading.

The gates to the outdoor handling pen should be strongly constructed and hung so that they close onto the sheep as they are penned. The fastenings should be about 500mm from the ground as this is where almost all of the pressure exerted by a pen filled with sheep will come. It is a great help to be able to step over the internal fences of the outdoor handling pen and a suggested height for these is 900mm. They should be of solid construction with occasional 'foot holes' built in to assist those who are unable to step over. The perimeter fences need to be a little higher at 1,200mm in order to contain the more athletic breeds.

Two things to bear in mind are that sheep will move uphill more freely than downhill, and towards light rather than towards dark, solid, high walls or buildings. You may also consider it worthwhile having a shallow tray or footbath where sheep requiring treatment for footrot or scald can be stood in a solution of zinc sulphate for a while.

If the sheep are kept on rented land where it is not possible to build a permanent handling area, a temporary one can be made using metal hurdles, securely held together. These are easily moved, and can be taken to wherever the sheep are, so that there is always an area in which they can be caught and held for inspection or treatment.

A temporary handling pen with funnel shaped approach

Chapter Four
Learning How to Handle Your Sheep

During the course of the year it is necessary to handle your sheep for dosing, vaccinating, foot trimming, etc. As described in the previous chapter, confine them in a small area so that the handler does not have to put on a rodeo show each time one needs to be caught! Do not be tempted to grab the wool as the sheep finds this very painful. In any event there is no wool on a newly shorn sheep.

Catching

There are three ways in which a sheep can be caught and restrained:

1. Firmly grasp a back leg just above the hock and lift the

leg off the ground.

2. Grasp the loose skin on the flank of the sheep just in front of a back leg and lift the leg from the ground.

3. Catch the lower jaw of the sheep in a cupped hand and lift the head above its natural horizontal position. Place the fingers of the other hand under the tail. It can now be moved backwards or forwards, but generally it is easier to move a sheep backwards, keeping the head up all the time.

If you wish to examine the teeth or read an ear number, it will be sufficient to back the sheep into a corner while still keeping control of the head, but you may find it easier to do this when the sheep is completely immobilised.

Immobilising

There are several ways of immobilising a sheep, and the following directions apply to right-handed people.

It can be done by sitting the sheep on its hindquarters and holding it between the knees, leaving both hands free for the examination. This will also be the position required when paring overgrown feet or treating footrot. To achieve this, having got the sheep into position with its chin held by a cupped hand, and standing on its left side, move the left hand around the neck so that the head is resting on the wrist and pull the sheep towards you. Place the left knee just behind the sheep's left shoulder and the right knee just in front of the sheep's left hip. Reach over and firmly grasp the loose skin in front of the sheep's right hind leg. Lean backwards and by using the knees as a pivot the sheep will roll onto its side on the knees of the operator. It can be lowered gently onto either its left or its right hindquarter. Avoid trying to make the sheep sit vertically on its tail as it finds this very uncomfortable.

(left) Catching by the hind leg

(right) Moving the sheep backwards or forwards

Another method of sitting the sheep onto its hindquarters

is to hold the sheep with the left hand cupped under its chin and place the right hand on its right hip bone. Move the sheep close to the legs, with the left knee behind its left shoulder and the right knee in front of its left hip, and pull its head round so far that it is looking back over its right shoulder. At the same time press firmly downwards with the right hand and move the right leg smartly away from contact with the sheep and it will collapse onto its hindquarter.

With experience this method of immobilising a sheep requires very little effort, but once the sheep is in position it is necessary to prevent its feet from coming in contact with the ground or fences etc. because if they do the sheep will kick and struggle as it attempts to regain the standing position.

Catching the lower jaw of the sheep in a cupped hand

Immobilising the sheep

There are a number

Immobilising the sheep by rolling it onto the knees of the operator of pieces of equipment on the market which can be used to immobilise sheep. The simplest of these is similar to a stretcher which can be placed at an angle against a fence. The animal is moved backwards until its rear end touches the frame and then the head is lifted until eventually the sheep is lying on its back on the stretcher. A rope is tied across the sheep just below its front legs and the operator is then free to use both hands to treat the sheep, as when trimming feet.

A Sheep Stretcher

Other items include a sheep 'cradle' which uses a series of clamps and levers to secure the sheep and to move it into an upside down position. This is helpful for anyone who has a back problem, but, as with the previous item, it has the disadvantage to the manual method in that the sheep has to be caught and moved to the equipment before it can be treated.

For heavily pregnant ewes who need assistance at lambing time, another method of immobilising is described on pages 95-96.

A mechanical device for immobilising sheep

It is possible to restrain sheep simply by passing the head through a loop of rope fixed to the side of the handling pen and placing the left knee just in front of the animal's left hip while pushing it against the side of the pen. This can be useful while dagging, crutching or treating blowfly strike in the tail area.

To examine the teeth, use the right hand to hold up the head and part the lips, using the thumb and index finger of the left hand to expose both the upper fibrous pad and the incisor teeth in the lower jaw. There are no incisor teeth in the upper jaw.

Chapter Five
Caring for Your Sheep

A dequate food and water are two essentials to the wellbeing of your sheep. The actual amount consumed will vary according to the type of sheep kept, and also from season to season, but try to maintain good bodily condition at all times. Be prepared to offer supplementary food when the nutritional requirements of the sheep are not being met because of poor quality or insufficient grazing. The condition required on any particular type of sheep can only be learned by experience, and a visit to a local market with a knowledgeable companion will be useful.

Supplementary Food

The type of supplementary food offered will depend on the time of year when the grass is in short supply and also on the type of sheep. Good quality hay made from grass cut at the early flowering stage, which has been baled and carted in dry weather and has no trace of mould, will usually provide for maintenance if fed at 2kg per day. It should be fed in hay racks to prevent waste. The rack should be large enough to allow the sheep to feed without overcrowding.

Ewes in the later stages of pregnancy will also require concentrates. Concentrates are highly nutritious food e.g. grain and various by-products from the edible oil seed crushing mills. These can be purchased in cube or pellet form to a guaranteed protein content from the local feed merchant. Introduce six weeks before lambing at the rate of 100g per day, increasing to 750g per day at lambing and afterwards. The concentrate is best provided as a compound mix of 17 percent protein. It is important that the compound is one specially formulated for sheep, as those prepared for other classes of livestock can contain minerals in proportions injurious to sheep. Similarly, sheep that are being fattened for meat or being prepared for show or sale, may require supplementary food.

Besides good quality hay and the concentrates, it may be necessary to provide more bulk in their diet. All kinds of root and cabbage crops are suitable, although one should watch out for the possibility of choking. NEVER feed green potatoes.

Sugar beet pulp is a very useful food. When fed dry the analysis compares with rolled oats. When soaked overnight in water, the extra bulk is beneficial in giving extra substance to animals being fed for show. If mangolds are available, they should be fed to ewes only after lambing. Any secondary shoots which have grown during storage should be trimmed off before feeding to wethers or rams, as they will cause urinary problems.

Supplementary food can be expensive, and it is important that the sheep obtain the maximum benefit from the food offered. All the feed troughs and water containers should be kept clean and free from contamination from faeces, mud, etc. and there should be sufficient trough space to allow all the sheep to feed in comfort. Hay should be fed from racks or hay boxes and kept dry at all times. If racks are used, try to prevent the sheep from standing directly underneath as the hay seeds and chaff will contaminate the fleeces thus reducing the value of the shorn wool, and they may also be responsible for eye problems.

If you offer young lambs supplementary feed in the form of pellets specially formulated for them, this can be done by fencing off an area to which only the lambs have access. Vertical posts which are spaced so that only the lambs can pass between them, together with a horizontal rail 450mm from the ground, will effectively exclude adult sheep.

Provide access to a balanced mineral supplement in a waterproof container at all times. Check with your vet whether there are any particular mineral deficiencies in your area, and if so how to overcome them.

Routine Tasks

In addition to the general requirements listed above, there are specific tasks which periodically require attention. See page 161 for the equipment to use in performing these tasks.

Foot Trimming

Foot trimming becomes necessary when the horny outer surface of the foot grows beyond the soft, rubbery sole of the foot. Sheep that are housed and those kept on damp, heavy land will require more frequent attention than those kept on drier and more abrasive soils. Feet that are not trimmed regularly can become compacted with soil and other debris, eventually causing lameness. To trim the foot, first immobilise the sheep and using straight-bladed secateurs or a sharp knife, carefully pare away the overgrown horn down to the level of the sole of the foot. Sometimes the pointed front end of the foot will have grown forwards and upwards. Be particularly careful when paring in this area as severe bleeding will occur if it is cut back too far.

Step One: Trimming overgrown feet with foot trimming shears

Steps Two and Three: Trimming overgrown feet with foot trimming shears

Dosing

In order to keep the sheep free from internal parasites, they will need to be dosed periodically with anthelmintics. These can be in the form of liquids, paste or capsules. Some are broad spectrum, which can deal with a number of different kinds of parasites, while others are more specific. It is important that the manufacturer's instructions for dosing are followed correctly, and as dosage depends on weight it will be necessary to weigh representative individuals to ensure that all the sheep receive the recommended amount of the anthelmintic. Give each sheep a temporary crayon mark as it is dosed to avoid giving a double dose to some and missing others completely!

Sheep can be dosed in the standing position. Hold the head in a horizontal position by placing a hand under the lower jaw and insert the instrument containing the anthelmintic into the corner of the mouth and onto the back of the tongue before releasing the dose. Various types of dosing instrument are available. These include:

- A trigger-operated gun which automatically delivers a pre-determined measured dose from a reservoir carried on the operator's back.
- A paste gun which delivers a measured dose.
- A narrow-necked bottle which will require filling with a measured dose between each sheep.
- A large plastic syringe (minus the hypodermic needle!) which is more suitable for young lambs.

If the sheep starts to cough violently, release the head at once to avoid choking.

Dosing with a trigger-operated gun

Dosing with a paste gun

Dosing a lamb with a syringe

Vaccination

It is possible to control a large number of diseases affecting sheep by preventative vaccines, and if these are given at the correct times and in the correct quantities, the immunity to the diseases can be passed from the ewe to the lamb via the colostrum, giving protection to the lamb for up to ten weeks. Depending on the type, the vaccine can be administered in one of three different ways.

1.   For a subcutaneous injection, lift a loose fold of skin with a thumb and forefinger, insert a hypodermic needle into the fold and release the vaccine by depressing the syringe. The preferred site for injections of small quantities of vaccine is high up on the neck, behind the ears. Quite often a small abscess or nodule will form at the injection site, and this can affect the subsequent value of the skin if present anywhere other than near the edge.

A Subcutaneous Injection

2.   Intramuscular injections should be given at a site where there is good muscle cover, e.g. into the hind leg. The needle is pushed straight into the muscle and the syringe contents released slowly.

3.   A live vaccine is applied to an area of bare

An Intramuscular Injection

skin between the front leg and the chest for protection against orf. The site should be clean but not disinfected otherwise the vaccine might be affected, and after application the site is lightly scratched so that the skin is broken to allow penetration of the vaccine. Gloves should be worn when using this vaccine as orf can also affect humans.

Dagging and Crutching

Both of these operations involve removing wool from the tail area of the sheep. In the spring when grass is growing quickly, the faeces are more liquid and can contaminate the wool. A build-up on the sheep can attract the blowfly to lay its eggs from which maggots will develop. Removing the wool helps to prevent this from happening, and it also avoids contamination of the fleece at shearing time.

A pair of sharp, short-bladed (100mm to 150mm) hand shears is used for dagging. The sheep is secured in a standing position by passing its head through a loop of rope attached to the side of the pen. Place a knee in front of the hip of the sheep, leaving both hands free to complete the operation.

Crutching involves taking off the wool from the area around the genitalia of the ewes prior to mating, but probably the main benefit will be at lambing time when the shorter wool makes visual inspection easier, particularly with longwoolled sheep. If wool is removed in front of the udder and from the front of the hind leg, it will give the newborn lamb easier access to the teats. To do this it will be necessary to turn the ewe as when trimming feet unless you possess a sheep cradle.

Shearing

In May or June all sheep that are more than one year old will need to be shorn. This is a skilled specialist operation and best left to shearing contractors. It might be possible to take the sheep to a neighbouring sheep farmer when his flock is being shorn, but the arrangements should be made well in advance as the shearers are usually very busy people.

Sheep are much less likely to suffer from stress at shearing if they are penned and kept away from food for at least twelve hours before they are to be shorn. They sit more easily on the shearing board, and the board stays clean and free from faeces. The wool must be dry before the sheep are penned under cover. Shorn fleeces which are wet, and contaminated with faeces, soil or vegetable matter will attract a penalty from the British Wool Marketing Board when the wool is sold, as will fleeces tied with cord, polypropylene or plastic twine.

If the flock consists of four or more ewes, some months before shearing it is necessary to register the flock with the British Wool Marketing Board, Registration Department, Oak Mills, Clayton, Bradford, West Yorkshire BD14 6JD. They will undertake to purchase the fleeces and will provide sacks to pack them in. Their agents will arrange collection after being notified that shearing has been completed. The British Wool Marketing Board requires that the fleeces are rolled in the correct manner. With shortwools the skin side of the fleece is on the outside, and with longwools the skin side is on the inside. The shorn fleece is laid out on a flat clean surface and any part of the fleece contaminated with faeces, mud, etc. removed. The loose belly wool, if clean, is placed on the centre of the fleece and the sides are folded to the middle before rolling from the tail end towards the neck. Make a small hole in the fleece and tuck the neck wool into this, and place the whole fleece in the sack provided.

Any skin cuts resulting from shearing will need treatment to assist healing. Keep a watch on any cuts that are being plagued by flies and treat again if necessary. The wound may be in a position where the sheep can strike it with its hind feet in an attempt to keep the flies away. This can soon result in an unpleasant open sore and it may become necessary to use lightweight sacking shaped like a horse rug to cover the body of the sheep. It should be inspected daily and dressed with an insecticidal cream. In extreme cases, putting the sheep into a darkened shed in the daytime will give it some respite from the unwelcome attention of flies.

Removing the wool from the tail end of the sheep using hand shears

Routine Inspections

All through the year a routine inspection of the flock is necessary, the frequency of the inspections varying with the time of year and the breed and condition of the sheep. Ideally it should never be less than twice a day, and more in the period preceding lambing. At this time the ewes are in good condition and heavy with lambs, and they can get on to their back when rolling and be unable to regain the standing position. This is common in early spring when showery weather alternating with drying sunshine and winds makes the sheep itchy. They roll onto their backs to relieve the itch and then get stuck in that position. If left like this, the continuing fermentation of food in the stomach and the pressure of the unborn lambs combine to restrict the breathing severely, eventually leading to suffocation and death.

In the period from early May until early November the sheep maggot fly is active and a careful watch is necessary for any sheep that are 'struck.' These will require prompt treatment so that any injury to the sheep caused by the maggots burrowing into the skin is minimised. A few weeks protection from the maggot fly is obtained when ewes are newly shorn and also when the lambs have been sprayed with an insecticidal dip.

Spend time watching the sheep without disturbing them so that any abnormal behaviour can be quickly recognised and if necessary acted upon.

Teeth

There are no incisor teeth in the sheep's upper jaw! Eight small incisor teeth appear soon after birth in the lower jaw. At about fifteen months of age the centre two are shed, and replaced by two larger, permanent incisors. At yearly intervals a tooth on either side of these will be shed and replaced by permanent ones, and the sheep is known consecutively as a two-tooth, four-tooth or six-tooth, according to the number of permanent incisor teeth present. At just over four years of age an adult sheep should have eight permanent incisor teeth and is then known as full-mouthed.

After four years the teeth continue to grow and will eventually be shed. The sheep is then said to be broken-mouthed. This may lead to feeding problems and unless

The Incisor teeth of a young lamb

Of a 15 month old sheep

Of a 3 year old sheep

special provision can be made any such ewes should be culled before mating.

Occasionally sheep are born with a lower jaw shorter or longer than normal. This can lead to feeding difficulties as the teeth will not meet the upper jaw pad correctly, and is an undesirable characteristic. Sheep with this condition are said to be 'undershot' or 'overshot' and should not be used for breeding. Careful examination of the teeth of any sheep which you consider buying is necessary.

Any problems with the molars, or back teeth, in either upper or lower jaws can usually be felt as hard lumps through the skin along the line of the jaw. Your vet will advise of any treatment necessary.

Body Condition Scoring

Condition scoring is an attempt to standardise how much fat and muscle a sheep is carrying by using the fingers to assess the degree to which the vertical and horizontal processes of the backbone are covered. The point were the assessment is made is in the region of the loin, behind the last rib and over the kidneys. It is scored on a scale of 0 to 5, and half points are also used.

Although the flock may be all of the same breed or cross, there will be considerable variation between individuals at any particular time. Between different breeds the variation will be even greater, and it will prove to be almost impossible to get all the animals into the same condition at the same time even if they are kept under the same conditions!

Assessing the body condition around the dock and over the loin

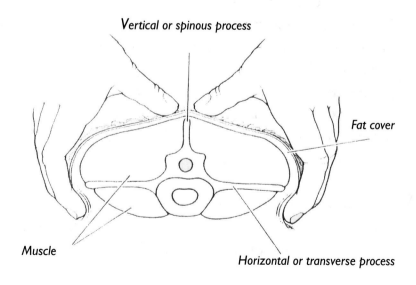

Vertical or spinous process

Fat cover

Muscle

Horizontal or transverse process

The position of the hands across the loin

Score 0 This indicates extreme emaciation with no fat or muscle detectable.

Conditon Score 1 - Lean

Score 1 The backbone feels very sharp in both the vertical and transverse processes, and muscle tissue in the angle between is very shallow with no fat cover.

Score 2 The muscle tissue is of sufficient depth to give the processes a smooth and rounded feeling, but there is little fat cover.

Conditon Score 3 - Good

Score 3 Individual spinous processes can be felt only by pressure and are smooth and well covered. The loin muscle is full with a moderate fat cover.

Score 4 The loin is full with a thick covering of fat and the spinous processes detectable only as a firm line. the ends of the transverse processes cannot be felt.

Conditon Score 5 - Fat

Score 5 The animal is very fat. There is a shallow groove in the fat cover over the vertical processes and the transverse processes are undetectable.

Chapter Six
Caring for the Breeding Flock

Care of the Breeding Ewe

A typical year for the breeding ewe begins a few weeks before mating takes place. The planned size and composition of the flock will have been completed, and the ewes brought on to a rising plane of nutrition, aiming for a body condition score of 3.5 at mating time. The prolificacy of the flock will be increased if the ewes are 'flushed' about three weeks before mating. This involves putting them onto better grazing if it is available, or feeding 200g of concentrates to each ewe each day until mating is completed. Flushing will result in more eggs being shed by the ovaries and more lambs being born. Any parasitic or foot problems will have been corrected, and any young sheep will have been given the appropriate vaccine in order to protect them from the clostridial group of diseases and from pasteurella pneumonia.

When the ram has joined the flock, and mating has begun, all unnecessary stress for the ewes should be avoided. It is best if the ram is fitted with a harness with a marker crayon which puts a colourful mark onto the rear of each ewe as she is mated, as this will enable you to keep a record of the mating date and work out the expected lambing date for each ewe. The gestation period is about 147 days.

When mating has been completed, remove the ram to a separate enclosure if possible. The condition of the ewes can now be allowed to drop back to a score of 3, although they should be given hay to appetite when the quality of the grazing deteriorates. If housing is available and the weather is bad, consider housing the ewes but try to ensure that the fleeces are dry before they move into the house for any period of time. Wet sheep will take a long time to dry when under cover.

Six weeks before lambing commences, begin concentrate feeding in addition to hay at the rate of 100g per sheep each day. Increase this amount weekly so that each ewe is receiving 750g daily when lambing commences. A booster injection of the vaccine against clostridial diseases should be given four weeks before they are due to lamb.

When each ewe has lambed place her in an individual pen made with hurdles and measuring 1.8m square. Any size smaller than this will expose the newborn lamb to the risk of being lain on when the ewe lies down, especially with multiple births. She should stay in the pen with her lambs for a few days until it is apparent that all is well with both ewe and lambs. The afterbirth will have come away shortly after lambing, and it should be collected and disposed of away from predators. The udder of the ewe will need to be inspected to ensure there is an adequate supply of milk for the lambs, and the lambs castrated and docked using rubber rings. When turning the ewes out of their individual pens with their lambs to join others that have already lambed, it is advisable to give each family an identification mark which will allow them to be recognised easily if for any reason they have to be segregated, or if a lamb loses sight of its mother and has to be reunited with her.

This is also a good opportunity to inspect each ewe's feet and trim if necessary, and also to give a dose of an anthelmintic to make sure she goes out worm-free. This dosing should continue at monthly intervals until the lambs are weaned.

During the lactation, and especially after weaning, keep a careful watch on the ewes for any sign of mastitis in overstocked udders, but do not be tempted to strip milk from ewes with healthy udders after weaning. This will only encourage the udder to produce more milk and will hold up the natural process of reabsorption.

If the ewe has successfully reared two or more lambs to weaning, she will very probably have lost condition and have a body condition score of around 2.5. Provided that she is healthy and that there is sufficient time to bring her up to a score of 3.5 before mating again, this is no cause for concern.

Before making up the breeding flock for the following year, a careful inspection of all the existing flock members is required to make sure that no unproductive passengers are being carried. Start with a look at the incisor teeth. Are the teeth present compatible with the age of the sheep? Do any sheep over four years of age have any incisors missing? If they have, and in all other respects they are sound and healthy, will facilities be available for them to have sufficient supplementary food in order to maintain their body condition, especially in the later stages of pregnancy? Feel the outside of the jaw along the site of the molars (back teeth) for any hard lumpy tissue which will indicate infected and possibly decaying teeth which will require veterinary attention. Next handle the udder, feeling for any lumps of hard tissue which will indicate chronic mastitis. A few weeks after weaning the udder should have returned to a soft, pliable consistency.

Any ewes with one or more of these defects or any adults that have not bred lambs when given the opportunity to do so for two consecutive years, should be given a separate identifying mark for culling. This also applies to any suffering from recurring chronic illnesses and those with chronic foot problems. Any ewes which have required a caesarean section operation to deliver their lambs will have only a 50 percent chance of breeding successfully in future years, and their retention as flock members should be carefully considered.

Following this inspection the sheep marked as culls can be marketed for meat when the price offered is favourable. Any surplus ewes suitable for breeding can be advertised for sale or taken to sheep auction sales which take place from mid-August until November.

Final decisions on the size and composition of the flock can then be made a few weeks before mating is due to begin. Any additions or replacements will have been made well in advance.

Selection and Care of the Ram

The breed of ram selected to be the sire of the flock is one of personal preference, but certain basic requirements in the conformation are common to all.

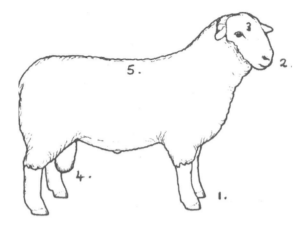

Look for:

1.   Good feet and straight legs with an easy walking action.
2.   Correct mouth with neither undershot nor overshot jaw.
3.   Bold eye and alert expression
4.   Large, even-sized testicles, firm to the touch.
5.   Long, straight back and good spring of rib.

Pay particular attention to the choice of ram, looking for one at the breed standard for size and weight. Always buy the best you can afford. If the ewes of the flock have a particular fault which needs correcting, beware of using a ram which is particularly good on that point while weak on others. Remember that the ram is responsible for half of the genetic make-up of his progeny.

Try to arrange for the ram to be kept separate from the rest of the flock until he is required for mating, but if possible give him company by providing him with a wether, or a ewe that you know has been successfully mated. A ram kept by himself without the company of other sheep can become aggressive, although this aggression can be minimised by fitting a face mask which restricts forward vision. Avoid making a pet of the ram by giving him titbits, as this too will encourage aggression.

Use a harness when the ram is with the ewes. The mark of a coloured crayon fitted to the harness will identify each ewe when mating takes place, and will let you know when to expect the lambs to be born. The harness should be fitted to the ram without the crayon

The ram harness

a few days before mating is due to start to allow it to settle into the fleece, and if necessary it can be tightened to give a good firm fit when the crayon is added. Check periodically that the harness and crayon-holder are not chafing.

The crayon should be changed after seventeen days to another colour as a check that mating has been successful, as this is the interval when the ewe's heat cycle recurs. If more than one or two ewes are marked by the second colour, having already been marked by the first one, it may be that the fertility of the ram is questionable, but wait a few days longer to see whether more ewes return for a second service before considering whether it is necessary to use another ram. Another change of colour should be made after a further seventeen days, by which time all the flock should have been mated.

The ram should always be kept in good condition, fit but not overfat (condition score 3.5 to 4), and in good health. Pay particular attention to the feet, inspect regularly and trim as necessary. A lame ram will be reluctant to work and this can mean a reduced lamb crop.

It is difficult to say with accuracy how many ewes a ram can successfully serve in a season, but an optimum number is around forty-five. Mature rams from very active breeds like the Wiltshire Horn are capable of serving many more. Avoid overworking ram lambs.

If the size of the flock does not justify the cost of purchasing a ram, it may be possible to hire one just for the mating season, or to have an arrangement with another flock owner where the ewes can be taken. Bringing other sheep in or sending sheep away for a short time can bring problems, e.g. footrot and parasitic infection. Have a careful look before exposing the sheep to the possibility of infection from outside sources.

Chapter Seven
Lambing

Lambing time can be the most rewarding, demanding and sometimes the most stressful time of the year for both sheep and shepherd. It is the culmination of all the efforts to ensure that the health, nutrition and general wellbeing of the sheep result in a successful increase in the size of the flock.

By far the largest proportion of ewes lamb successfully unaided but a small number do need assistance. The way in which the assistance is given can vary a great deal, but the methods described in this book have been developed and proven over many years by us to give acceptable results.

It will not be possible to save every lamb that is born, as some may be still-born, but the golden rules are:

* Have your lambing kit to hand well before lambing commences, and also the telephone number of your vet.
* Practise as high a standard of hygiene as possible under the circumstances prevailing.
* Be patient. Do not rush to assist even in a normal birth, especially with ewes lambing for the first time. It is possible for the whole process to last for four hours and still result in a normal, natural birth.

The Lambing Kit

You may require the following lambing aids:

A lubricant

This is for use when it is necessary to assist a ewe by an internal examination and/or manipulation of the unborn lamb. This can be in the form of a mild antiseptic oil or cream, or soap and water. Soap flakes are particularly good.

A metre length of thin cord

By tying a loop at each end this can be used to secure an unborn lamb's feet or head and will make it easier to pull the lamb from the ewe should this become necessary. The cord should be stored in a weak antiseptic solution in an unbreakable container.

A Lambing Aid

This is a Y-shaped plastic tube containing a retractable plastic covered cord. It can be used, with experience, to secure the unborn lamb's head and feet together inside the ewe and therefore enable the operator to withdraw the lamb from the ewe in a normal presentation position.

A Navel Dressing

This dressing dries the lamb's navel very quickly and thus prevents harmful organisms gaining entry to the lamb, particularly the bacteria that cause joint-ill and liver abscess. The dressing can be: tincture of iodine antibiotic aerosol, a very weak solution of copper sulphate.

Ideally the dressing should be kept in a wide-necked container so that the navel cord and surrounding area can be immersed by holding the lamb vertically by the front legs and pressing the container gently against the lamb.

A Supply of Colostrum

It is absolutely essential that newborn lambs are given colostrum as their first feed. Colostrum is a sticky yellow substance usually present in the udder when the lamb is born. It is a rich source of energy and also a laxative; provided the ewe has been given the appropriate vaccines it will also contain antibodies which will give the lamb protection from specific diseases through the early stages of its life.

If the ewe has not produced any colostrum, or if there are more than two lambs, a supply can be obtained from a ewe whose lambs have died at birth or from one side of the udder of a ewe that has produced a single lamb.

If neither of these sources is available, colostrum from a newly kidded goat or a newly calved cow can be substituted, but unless the animals have been vaccinated beforehand it will be necessary to vaccinate the new-born lamb against clostridial diseases.

Colostrum can be frozen in small packs of 200ml for storage. It must be properly thawed and heated to 40°C before use.

A final alternative is to use a ewe colostrum replacer made up according to the manufacturer's instructions.

A Stomach Tube with Syringe
This is necessary when giving colostrum to weakly lambs.

Baby feeding bottles and teats
Sometimes the ewe's supply of milk in the first few days is insufficient for her lambs. If so, after the initial feed of colostrum, the lambs will need supplementary feeding with milk from other ewes or with a good-quality ewe milk replacer.

Rubber Rings

These are used together with the appropriate pliers for tailing and castrating.

Pessaries

These are either antibiotic or antiseptic and are placed in the uterus of the ewe after her lamb has been delivered following internal manipulation. They can be obtained from your vet.

A Hypodermic Syringe and Needles

These are necessary for injecting the ewes and lambs.

A Quantity of Magnesium Fortified Calcium Borogluconate

This is injected subcutaneously into ewes which collapse suddenly with hypomagnesaemia (magnesium deficiency) or hypocalcaemia (milk fever).

A Wire or Plastic Support for Vaginal Prolapse

A vaginal prolapse usually occurs during the few weeks before lambing. Normally it first appears as a pinkish rose-shaped object, and may not be showing all the time. If the condition deteriorates and the prolapse gets bigger, then the ewe may have difficulty in urinating. This causes strain, and in the extreme condition the wall of the vagina may break and consequently the intestines escape through the hole. When it reaches this stage there is no cure and the vet should be called to destroy the ewe. The wire support, which has loops to secure it to the fleece of the ewe, should be inserted into the vagina when it is apparent that the prolapse is not going to go back on its own. It can be left in position until lambing is well advanced and the lamb is about to be born.

Stock Markers

It is advisable to have several different colours available to mark lambs or ewes needing to be identified temporarily.

A Halter

Occasionally a ewe will reject one lamb of her twins or triplets and a short spell tied with a halter will usually overcome this problem. The halter rope should be tied to a corner of the pen, high enough and short enough to prevent the ewe from turning round, but still allowing her to feed and drink easily. It is also a good idea to put a length of rubber tubing on the part of the halter which passes under the jaw. This will prevent the halter from becoming tight and therefore causing chafing.

A torch with a spare battery
Disposable plastic gloves
The vet's telephone number

The Lambing Kit:

(1) lubricant; (2) baby feeding bottle and teats; (3) stock marker; (4) calcium borogluconate; (5) navel dressing; (6) pessaries; (7) torch; (80 lambing ropes; (9) castrating pliers with rubber rings; (10) frozen colostrum; (11) stomach tube with syringe; (12) hypodermic syringe with needles; (13) vaginal support; (14) sheep halter; (15) lambing aid.

Lambing: Signs and Observations

The first indication that a ewe is about to commence lambing is that she behaves abnormally. Spend time watching normal behaviour in ewes so that any abnormal behaviour can be recognised.

The ewe will select a spot for her lambs to be born, and if she is driven away from it she will return at the earliest opportunity. She will become agitated, often pawing the

Finding a spot to lamb

The ewe strains

Curling her lip

ground and bleating softly. She will also lie down and get up again at frequent intervals. It is advisable to allow the ewe to remain at the site she has chosen, provided that it is sheltered, safe and dry. She is more likely to get on with the job of producing her lambs than if she is moved to another site or put in a small pen. Some ewes do not like an audience at close quarters when lambing and may give up attempting to lamb if anyone is near.

Labour

The ewe begins to strain very obviously as the birth commences and she

90

lies down, often with her legs stretched out to one side. She often raises her head, closes her eyes and curls her top lip. The 'waterbag' is a transparent membrane containing the birth fluid. It may burst inside the ewe, but usually appears outside and bursts within a few minutes.

The waterbag appears

A Normal Presentation

A Normal Presentation

With continued straining the lamb's nose and both front feet will appear. Often they will be enclosed in a transparent membrane. Slowly the body of the lamb will slide from the ewe. If the transparent membrane is still intact, prompt action is necessary to remove it otherwise the lamb will be unable to breathe and will suffocate.

The lamb will kick and cough and then the ewe will stand and turn to lick it. This has the combined effect of drying the lamb, establishing a bond between lamb

Early signs

Selecting a spot

The ewe begins to strain

and ewe and stimulating the lamb's circulation. This is a time of rapid heat loss in the lamb, particularly in inclement weather, and careful watch should be kept to see that it does not suffer from hypothermia due to exposure. If the ewe is reluctant to start licking, place the lamb at her head and rub some of the birth fluid over her nostrils.

After the birth of the lamb, the ewe can be moved to a sheltered position by holding the lamb by front or back legs and drawing it slowly in the direction that you wish the ewe to travel. It is very important that the lamb stays at ground level where the ewe can see it and can continue licking and smelling it as she moves. If she loses sight of the lamb she will return to the spot she chose for the birth.

Moving the ewe and newborn lambs

Before leaving the ewe with her lamb, gently draw the thumb and forefinger down her teats to break the seal at the end so that the lamb can easily obtain the colostrum. The afterbirth should come away from the ewe after the birth(s) have been completed. Some ewes will attempt to eat the afterbirth, but it should be cleared away as it can distract the ewe from caring for her lamb. It will also attract predators – dogs, foxes and carrion crows. If the afterbirth becomes covered with straw and is allowed to decompose for some time, the smell of decomposition can be most unpleasant. It should be properly disposed of by burying.

Checking the udder

The afterbirth or cleansing coming away

The Normal Birth

The nose and both front feet appear

The lamb slides from the ewe

The ewe licks the lamb

Whether to Assist the Birth

Patience is a virtue! Do not rush to assist the ewe even in a normal birth. If, after an hour or so of labour commencing, nothing can be seen of the lamb and no progress is being made, then quietly catch the ewe. Insert one or two fingers into the vagina and try to identify any part of the lamb which you can touch. If an assistant is available to hold the ewe, this can be done while the ewe is still standing. Otherwise, it will be necessary to immobilise her by laying her down on her right side. This can be done by standing or kneeling at her left side and pulling her head round towards you while simultaneously reaching under her and grasping her right hind leg, then pulling it through in front of her udder towards you.

This is a move that can be practised at any time of the year, prior to the lambing season. Use a small sheep and progress to a larger one as you become proficient. The ewe will collapse onto her right side and your left hand and left leg can be used to keep her immobilised while the right hand makes a preliminary examination.

Remember that a normal birth can take up to four hours and if your examination shows that no part of the lamb can be felt and entry to the uterus is dry and restricted, then release the ewe and wait a while before making another examination. If after three hours no further progress is being made, do be patient and do not force an entry. Seek help from your vet.

Immoblising the pregnant ewe

Ringwomb

This is a condition where the cervix, or entrance to the uterus, fails to dilate. It can be recognised when a preliminary examination reveals, as the name implies, a tight inelastic ring at the entrance to the uterus. Do not force an entry but contact your vet.

An Introduction to Keeping Sheep
Gallery of Breeds

" Sheep are seldom boring and rarely profitable!" to quote a well known farmer. In spite of this, (or because of it?) some twenty million of the creatures are kept in this country. Endearing and infuriating all at the same time, they provide a magnetic interest for those who allow themselves to be attracted to them. Treat them well and the rewards will be many.

The Shortwools

The Shortwools include the Down breeds which were developed in the southern half of England by using a Southdown ram on ewes of various local breeds.

Southdown

Hampshire Down

Dorset Down

Oxford Down

Suffolk

Kerry

Polled
Dorset

The Longwools

Generally speaking the Longwools are larger sheep which mature more slowly than the Shortwools. They were more popular when families were larger and consequently larger joints of mutton were required. Their fleeces provided an income from the relatively poorer hill areas of the Cotswolds and the Yorkshire and Lincolnshire Wolds. These areas are the homes of the Cotswold, the Leicester and the Lincolnshire Longwool breeds. The Longwool group also includes the Romney Marsh, which originates from the low-lying area of that name in Kent.

Border Leicester

Devon and
Cornwall
Longwool

Dartmoor

Wensleydale

The Hill Breeds

The hardy and thrifty hill breeds are smaller sheep than either of the two previous categories and they have evolved a habit of scattered grazing spreading themselves thinly on the ground so that there is less competition for the available grazing. When enclosed in a lowland situation they regard a field boundary as a challenge to see what lies beyond, as they believe the grass is always greener on the other side! They occupy a uniqe position in the sheep industry in that their distribution covers a huge area of high land which is largely unsuitable for any other type of farming.

Blackface

Herdwick

Scottish
Blackface

Torwen

Badgerfaced

Swaledale

Black Welsh
Mountain

Wiltshire Horn

Jacob

Rough Fell

Shetland

Rare Breeds

These are mainly British breeds that have lost their popularity. Many traditional breeds were developed by farmers to meet the particular requirement of a small local area, but with a wider dissemination of knowledge and an efficient transport system, sheep could be taken far from their home base to perform as well as, if not better than, they did at home. These rare breeds are now being saved from extinction mainly by interested hobby farmers and rare breed establishments.

Manx Loghtan

Portland

Llanwenog

Breeds from Abroad

n recent years many brees have been imported into the UK from various parts of the world, often to improve conformation and carcase quality.

Charollais

Rouge de l'Oest

Merino

New Zealand Southdown

Texel

Bleu du Maine

*Keeping the ewe
immobilised*

Malpresentations

Unfortunately a number of malpresentations can occur, and if the examination shows that the lamb is being presented in a position other than normal, then one of the procedures on the following pages is called for. **If you feel that you are unable to cope with these malpresentations, seek help from your vet before attempting to proceed beyond your initial examination.**

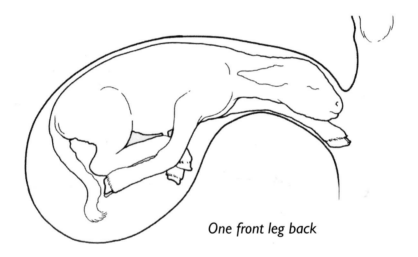

One front leg back

One front leg back

This position means that only one front leg is forward and that the other front leg is lying alongside the lamb's body inside the ewe. To deliver the lamb, the visible hoof should be gripped firmly and the leg pulled out of the ewe in line with her backbone. Run one or two fingers around the top of the lamb's head to ease it from the vagina. When this has been done, pull the leg and head towards the ewe's hocks, maintaining an even pressure until the lamb has been delivered.

The visible hoof should be gripped firmly

Pull the leg and head towards the ewe's hocks

Both Front legs back

In this case ease the lamb's head right outside the ewe and slide the right hand down the left side of the lamb's neck, feeling for its left shoulder and left front leg. Crook a finger behind the leg and pull it up in line with the lamb's neck. Deliver the lamb by pulling the foot and head downwards towards the ewe's hocks. It is not necessary to re-insert your hand into the ewe to bring up the other front leg.

Both front legs back

Ease lambs head out of the ewe

Locate a front leg and pull to the outside. Deliver as with one front leg back

If the ewe has been unattended and in labour for some time, she may have succeeded in getting the lamb's head out of the vagina. When this happens its head and tongue may appear very swollen but the swelling will quickly subside once the lamb has been delivered.

Hind legs first

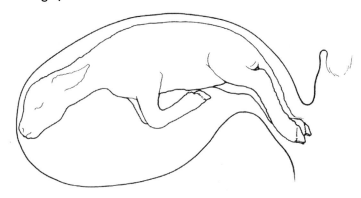

Hind Legs First

If, on examination, only two feet can be felt and no head, and the points of the hooves are on the underside, then feel up the legs for the lamb's hocks. If they are present grip them firmly and quickly deliver the lamb by pulling it out in line with the ewe's backbone. It might be necessary to put a cord around the feet of the lamb to enable you to get a better grip on them, but it is important that the lamb is delivered quickly. If not, there is a possibility that it will attempt to breathe when the umbilical cord

Pulling the lamb out hind legs first

breaks while the head is still inside the ewe.

It will then take the birth fluid into its lungs and may suffocate. If you suspect that this has happened, hold the lamb by its hind legs and swing it violently backwards and forwards in an attempt to expel the fluid and mucus from its lungs. Clear away any mucus from the lamb's mouth and check whether its heart is beating by gently pressing on its rib cage immediately behind its shoulder. If the heartbeat is present but the lamb is not breathing, mouth-to-mouth resuscitation may help. If the need arises, don't be put off by the appearance of the lamb – there is virtually no taste to the birth fluid!

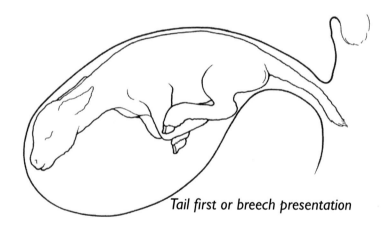

Tail first or breech presentation

Tail First or Breech Presentation

An indication that the ewe is attempting a breech birth will be the appearance of the lamb's tail. Gently push the hindquarters of the lamb back inside the ewe and reach for its hind legs. Pull both hind legs up and outside the ewe, and then quickly pull the lamb out in line with the ewe's backbone. If necessary, swing it and proceed as with the hind legs presentation to expel fluid and mucus from the lungs.

Dealing with a breech presentation

HHead back, both front feet forward

Head Back, Both Front Feet Forward

This is the most difficult presentation to deal with. Firstly, identify positively that the feet are front feet by noting that the points of the hooves are uppermost and feeling for a knee. Do not under any circumstances pull on these legs hoping that a head will follow, as if the head is turned back, pulling the legs will force the head even further back.

Instead put the lamb's feet in the palm of your hand and, after attaching a thin, disinfected rope to each, push them back inside the ewe. As soon as it is possible to do so, push them down so the legs are under the body of the lamb. Locate the curved body of the lamb and pull the head forward by putting the thumb and forefinger in the eye sockets. Bring the head right outside the ewe, using the rope to bring up its legs at the same time. Deliver the lamb by pulling its head and legs towards the ewe's hocks.

Bringing the head forward

This is an occasion when the lambing aid can come into its own. It can be used to snare the lamb's head and legs after locating them inside the ewe, and also for pulling them through the pelvis to the outside.

Twin Lambs Presented Together

This can be a puzzling situation for beginners. If two heads and some or all of the front legs are presented together, it will be necessary to push one head and all the legs back inside the ewe. Bring one head to the outside before going back for one front leg, making sure that it belongs to the same lamb as the head! Deliver the lamb by pulling the head and feet downwards towards the ewe's hocks.

In all other cases of mixed-up presentations, try to identify positively any part of a lamb that you can touch. If a head is presented, then work with this one. If at any time it is difficult to move the lamb inside the ewe, it sometimes helps to roll the ewe over onto her left side and then back again onto the right.

Guarding against Infection

In all cases of assisted birth an antiseptic or antibiotic pessary should be inserted into the ewe when all the lambs have been delivered. Additionally, an intra-muscular injection of a long-acting antibiotic should be given to prevent infection. This is obtainable from your vet.

Dead Lambs

You may find that you are having to assist in the birth of a dead lamb. This can be a difficult and unpleasant task, especially if the lamb is beginning to decompose. The dead lamb will feel dry to the touch and the natural lubrication of the birth will be absent. Use copious amounts of lubrication, soap and water for preference.

If you feel you are unable to cope with this, consult your vet. He will also advise you on the use of long-acting antibiotics and pessaries.

Care of the Lamb

The first few days of a lamb's life are critical to its future development, and a careful watch should be kept on all newborn lambs so that any potential problems can be recognised early.

Following a successful birth the ewe normally begins to lick the lamb clean and dry. The lamb gets to its feet after a few minutes, makes its way to the ewe's udder and beings to suck vigoroughly. The ewe and lamb should be placed in a small pen (1.8m x 1.8m) on a clean bed of straw. This will prevent the lamb from straying, especially in the case of a multiple birth where the ewe might have to care for several lambs. The lamb's umbilical cord should be dressed (see the lambing kit list) to guard against infection.

If the lamb has been born outside in inclement weather, it may be suffering from hypothermia, or chilling, and finding it difficult or impossible to get to its feet. Help to stimulate circulation by rubbing the lamb briskly with a dry towel, and introduce it to the ewe's milk by opening its mouth and inserting a teat, gently squeezing it to give the lamb a taste. This task is made easier by casting the ewe onto her side, and then by leaning over her and placing an ankle over her neck, which will leave both hands free to handle lamb and teat. An elbow gently placed into the flank of the uppermost leg of the ewe will prevent a kick in the face! If the lamb is reluctant to suck, it can sometimes be stimulated by scratching its tail head.

Dressing the umbilical cord

Feeding with a stomach tube

Feeding with a syringe

Feeding with a bottle

If it is still cold, wet and lethargic but able to hold up its head unaided, it can by fed using a stomach tube. To do this, sit comfortably with the lamb on the lap. Introduce the tube minus the syringe into the lamb's mouth and gently slide it into the stomach, making sure that it is in the oesophagus and not the windpipe. Place two fingers across the underside of the neck and if the tube can be felt, it is going down the oesophagus. If not, it is in the windpipe and should be withdrawn immediately. If the lamb shows no sign of discomfort and chews the tube when it is in position, this indicates that it is in the stomach and all is well.

In a large lamb all but two inches of the stomach tube can be introduced. The syringe should be filled with colostrum taken from the ewe and placed on the end of the tube. Depress the plunger of the syringe very slowly and repeat the process until the lamb has received between 100 and 200ml, repeating this four hours later if necessary. As soon as the lamb begins to suck unaided, place it at the ewe's teat.

Ensure that the lamb gets an adequate supply of at least one litre of colostrum during the first twenty-four hours of its life. If the ewe has no colostrum, use a baby's feeding bottle to give it from another source (see page 85).

If, after twenty-four hours, the ewe has no milk or insufficient milk, feed the lamb with milk from another ewe or use a good quality ewe milk replacer.

Apply a strict hygiene routine to the stomach tube, syringe, bottle and teat used to feed lambs, and thoroughly clean and sterilise between each feed.

If it becomes necessary to warm a lamb by an artificial heat source, several methods can be used. An infra-red lamp is useful, but take care to see that it is far enough away from the lamb (a minimum of 1.2m) to prevent scorching or burning. A drawback to this method is that when dry the lamb takes on a different smell and because the mother of a newborn lamb identifies it by smell alone she sometimes refuses to accept that it belongs to her. A way around this problem is to suspend the lamp above the lamb in a small fenced off corner of the pen where the ewe can still see and smell the lamb but where she cannot be burned.

A domestic hot air blower can be used to blow warm air onto the lamb lying in a box or confined space, as can the oven of a domestic cooker at a low temperature, but remember to leave the oven door open!

If no artificial heat source is available, a hay box can be used to revive a lamb suffering from exposure. Use soft hay to make a deep nest inside a container such as a large dustbin or forty-five gallon drum. Place the lamb in the nest and cover with clean hessian sacks or more hay before putting a lid on the container. An hour or so later the lamb will usually be standing on the sacks or hay and calling for food.

Any lamb which is cold and lethargic when several hours old and already dry should not be subjected to artifical heat. Give a feed of colostrum from a baby's feeding bottle or through a stomach tube if the lamb is reluctant to suck.

Castrating

When it is apparent that all is well – the lambs are receiving an adequate supply of milk and the ewe is mothering properly – the ram lambs can be castrated. The simplest way for the beginner to do this operation is to use rubber rings and the appropriate pliers, called elastrators. By law this method is permissible only during the first week of a lamb's life, and by persons over seventeen years of age. First check for abnormalities. The lamb may be suffering from a scrotal hernia, when a part of the intestine is present in the scrotum with the testicles, and can be detected as a soft, spongy mass. Lambs with this condition will die if castrated. Sometimes either one or both of the testicles have not descended into the scrotum. If only one has descended, do not castrate. The tail should be left long for identification while waiting for the testicles to come down normally.

Kneel or sit with the lamb lying on its back between your legs and facing away from you. Place a rubber ring on the elastrator, stretch the ring open and draw the scrotum through it. Close the ring on the scrotum and then open it just sufficiently to allow a testicle to be eased through it into the scrotum, using the free hand (see illustrations on facing page). Close it again and repeat the procedure for the second testicle. Make sure that the rubber ring is well below the rudimentary teats and that both testicles are secured before removing the elastrator from the ring.

At sixteen to twenty weeks of age an uncastrated ram lamb becomes sexually active and can be a nuisance if left with the flock. Either segregate it or send it to market.

Steps in castrating

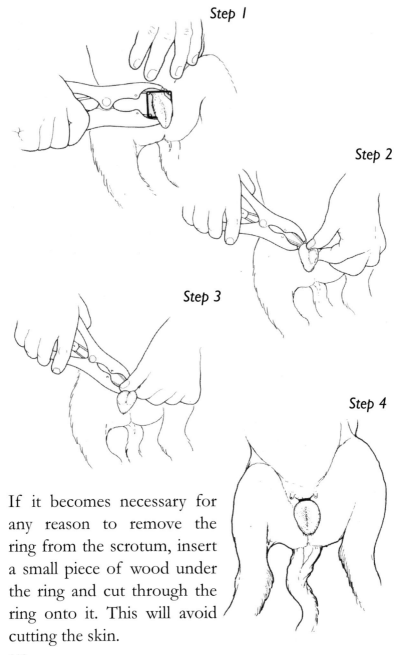

Step 1

Step 2

Step 3

Step 4

If it becomes necessary for any reason to remove the ring from the scrotum, insert a small piece of wood under the ring and cut through the ring onto it. This will avoid cutting the skin.

Docking

To dock the lamb place a ring on the elastrator, open the ring and pass the tail through it. Before closing the ring on the tail, ensure that sufficient tail is left above the ring to cover the anus of ram lambs and the vulva of ewe lambs. (This is required by law).

After these operations both ram and ewe lambs suffer some discomfort and will roll around on the ground for a short time. Because of this it is advisable to do the job either on a clean straw bed or on a clean grass field. The discomfort soon passes and the lambs are soon behaving normally again.

Docking

Fostering Lambs

Occasionally it may be necessary to foster an orphan lamb onto a ewe that has lost her lamb, or to foster a lamb from a multiple birth onto a ewe that has produced only a single lamb. There are several ways of doing this.

Skinning

In the case of a dead lamb remove the skin, trying if possible to leave the holes for the legs intact. Place the skin with the tail still attached onto the lamb to be fostered, putting the legs through the holes left in the skin so that it covers all the body except the head and ears. If necessary, use string to join the skin to make a good fit. As a safeguard, put a halter on the ewe and tie her to the corner of a small pen. Tie the rope at a height that will allow the ewe to lie down in comfort but will not permit her to turn round or step over the rope. She will usually accept the lamb straight away, but it may be necessary for the first few days to shorten the halter rope every few hours and stand by while the lamb is encouraged to suck.

Using Birth Fluids From a Newborn Lamb

To foster a lamb onto a ewe that is producing a single lamb takes rather more expertise. Firstly, be present at the birth. Immediately afterwards, before the ewe stands up or sees her own lamb, press a hand onto the abdomen just in front of the udder to see whether there is another lamb in the uterus. If there is, it can be felt as a firm, solid mass and as an additional check put one finger into the vagina to feel for any lamb about to be born. If no other lamb is present, keep the ewe in a lying position and if necessary wrap her head in a cloth so that she is blindfolded. She will then lie quietly.

Collect the lamb to be fostered, and using string, tie a front leg to the diagonally opposite back leg so that it is unable to stand. The foster lamb will usually be dry, but if it too is newborn and still wet, rub it briskly with a dry towel to dry it as much as possible. Use all the birth fluids available from the newly lambed ewe and her lamb, if necessary squeezing fluid from the legs and nose of the lamb, to saturate the foster lamb. Place the foster lamb at the ewe's head and remove the blindfold. Take away the ewe's own newborn lamb for about twenty minutes while the ewe licks the foster lamb, before returning it to its mother. The attempts of the foster lamb to stand while its legs are tied simulate the efforts of the newborn lamb trying to get to its feet. Wait another twenty minutes before untying the legs. During this time the newborn lamb, if it is healthy and normal, will have got to its feet and taken its first feed of colostrum from the ewe. Keep the ewe and lambs in a small pen for a few days to check that all is well and that both lambs are thriving.

Lamb Adopters

These are boxes or crates which constrain a ewe in such a way that she cannot see or smell the lamb which is being fostered. The lamb has access to the ewe at all times and also has a safe area where it cannot be trampled on or kicked and butted by the ewe. The apparatus can be purchased or made up at home using plywood. It consists of a stall approximately 1 metre wide and 1.2 metres long, with a slot at the front just wide enough to take the ewe's neck comfortably, but narrow enough to prevent her from withdrawing her head when placed in it. A rail on either side of the ewe prevents sideways movement and provides the lamb with a safe, draughtproof area.

The theory is that after the milk has passed through the lamb for a few days, the lamb will take on the smell of the ewe and she will eventually recognise it and accept it as her own. This method is more successful with ewes that have only recently lambed. After release keep both ewe and lamb in a small pen until it is seen that all is well.

Ewes which are normally placid creatures can behave violently towards lambs which are not their own. Sometimes a ewe which has given birth to twins will reject one for no apparent reason. If both lambs are strong and active, tie the ewe to a corner of the pen using a halter, and after a few days she will usually accept both lambs. Try taking both lambs away for about half an hour. When they are returned she will usually be so pleased to see them that she allows both of them to suckle her.

After tailing, castrating and any fostering have been successfully completed, several ewes with their lambs can be grouped together in a small enclosure. Use a stock marker aerosol to identify lambs with their mothers by marking them on both sides of the body with a similar number or symbol.

From now on, given an adequate supply of milk and grass, the lambs should thrive. Dose with a broad-spectrum anthelmintic at six weeks of age and again at monthly intervals to keep parasitic worms under control. If supplementary feeding is needed for the lambs, it can be started when they are around ten days of age. It can be in the form of pellets specially formulated for lambs or as a coarse mix containing ingredients which the lambs find particularly attractive – a kind of lamb muesli! Both will be available from your feed merchant. From an early age the lambs will also eat hay which, as is the case for all classes of sheep, must be of good quality.

The feed for the lambs should be made available to them via a lamb creep through which the ewes cannot pass. It should be offered to them ad lib until they are eating around 300g a day. After that they should have a single feed each morning, the amount being dictated by the quality and the quantity of the grazing and the condition of the lambs. The feed, particularly when offered ad lib, should be protected from the weather and the lambs prevented from standing in the troughs when feeding.

Clean water should always be available to both ewes and lambs.

All the sheep are at risk of fly strike between April and November when they should be checked at least twice a day (see blowfly strike in Chapter 8). Short-term protection can be provided by dipping in an insecticidal dip.

If lambs are intended for the meat market, periodic weighing is required. With small numbers this can be done using bathroom scales or a sling or container and spring balance. The optimum weight for marketing is between 32 and 40kg liveweight, which will give a carcase of approximately 48 percent of that weight, depending on the degree of finish or fatness. Lambs from the smaller breeds of sheep and some of the rare breeds will be ready for market at lighter weights.

Hand Rearing Orphan and Surplus Lambs

Day One
It is essential that new-born lambs receive a minimum of one litre of colostrum or colostrum replacer during the first twenty-four hours of life (see page 108). It is important to thoroughly clean and sterilise all the utensils

used in rearing orphan lambs.

Days Two to Nine

Introduce a good quality ewe milk replacer of preferably 30 percent fat content, mixed with water in accordance with the manufacturer's instructions. Feed warm in four feeds to a total of one litre per lamb per day, using a bottle with teat attached.

It is possible to rear lambs on ewe milk substitute fed cold. It should be available ad lib and should be offered via teats fixed to the side of the pen, connected by plastic tubing to a supply of milk outside the pen. It is very important that the teats when fixed in position are above the level of the milk substitute in the container. The lambs will need to be taught how to use this feeding method by holding them onto the teat for the first few feeds. An infra-red lamp suspended not less than 1 to 2 metres above the pen will be appreciated by them.

Days Ten to Nineteen

Introduce hay and concentrate feeding. As always, the hay should be of top quality and in order to tempt the lambs to eat concentrates, offer a small amount of flaked maize initially. Small pellets of compound feed purchased from your feed merchant can be introduced gradually. Restrict warm milk to two feeds per day.

Days Twenty to Forty-two

Continue with hay and concentrate feeding. Provide

clean water. The water container and any feed troughs used should be scrupulously clean and set up in such a way that the lambs cannot foul them with their feet or with urine or dung.

Day Forty-three onwards

The lambs can be weaned and turned out onto clean grass. Feed concentrates twice daily at the rate of 250g per lamb per feed. They will be ready for marketing when they reach 32 to 40kg. The smaller breeds may be ready before they reach this weight.

Chapter Eight
Some Common Diseases Affecting Sheep

It is always alarming to read about the numerous diseases to which sheep, like any other animal, can succumb, but good management, sensible fencing, anticipation of potential troubles and quick reaction will ensure that disasters rarely happen.

Blowfly Strike

This is probably the most common and troublesome of all diseases during the warmer months from April to November. The green or blue blowfies, which are slightly larger than houseflies, actively seek sites where they can lay their eggs and where the hatching maggots can obtain food. The fly finds the sheep particularly

Sheep showing signs of flystrike

attractive when there are faeces contaminating the tail area, but even without this the natural smell of the sheep is sufficient to entice the fly to lay its eggs on the wool, and any open wounds can suffer the same fate. The eggs hatch in a few hours and the maggots start feeding by burrowing into the skin. The debris they create attracts more flies, and within a very short time the area affected rapidly increases in size.

However, long before this happens, the behaviour of the sheep will indicate to the observant shepherd that it requires attention. Sheep which have newly hatched maggots will be irritated by them and will waggle their tails vigorously. They may stamp the ground with a hind foot and twist the whole body from side to side while holding the head high in the air. The sheep must be caught and examined carefully. Apply a combined insecticide and antiseptic to the site of the maggots and also the surrounding wool to catch any that attempt to escape, rubbing the medication into the fleece with the fingertips.

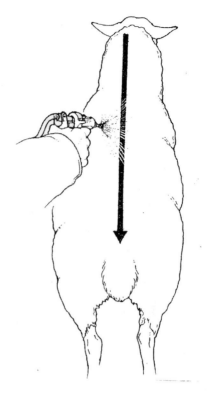

If the strike is left untreated, the next indication will be a dark stain on the surface of the wool which is caused by the excreta from the maggots. By now the sheep will be feeling very sick and

Preventing flystrike

may be lying by itself under a tree or hedge. If moved it will stand with its head lowered and quickly lie down again.

In July and August the blowfly often lays eggs on the back of the sheep near the shoulders. When the maggots develop there, the sheep will stand with its head lowered and appear to be very sick. The tail waggling and body twisting are absent and one of the few visual signs is the tell-tale dark stain starting on the back and running down on to the shoulders. This appears after the maggots have been feeding for a day or two. Try to recognise the situation and deal with it before this.

Any sheep which have footrot are also at risk, as the distinctive smell of footrot attracts the blowfly to lay its eggs, and the resulting maggots penetrate the under-run hoof. Trim off the under-run sole and saturate with an insecticidal and antiseptic dressing.

Adult sheep are at risk of fly strike from late April until they are shorn. They are then free from infection until the wool has grown to around 20cm, after which they can be protected for a few weeks by using a pour-on preparation such as Vetrazin. Lambs, unless they are shorn, are at risk all through the summer, but they too can be protected by using a pour-on preparation.

Blowfly strike is less likely to occur if preventative measures are taken routinely. Wool contaminated after lambing or as a consequence of diarrhoea should be cut off. Shearing is usually carried out in June but in exceptionally mild weather in the south of England it can be brought forward to the end of April. Clean, freshly shorn sheep are unlikely to suffer fly strike.

Sheep Scab

Sheep scab is caused by a mite which burrows into the skin and causes intense itching, along with rapid loss of wool and condition, and it requires immediate attention. If an infection is suspected, contact the vet immediately. He will be able to suggest the most effective treatment. Scab is contagious and will rapidly spread through the flock if untreated. It is still a notifiable disease and unfortunately has become much more prevalent since annual dipping of sheep ceased to be compulsory. The disease will get into the flock only if there is very close contact with infected sheep or recently contaminated equipment, so it is wise to isolate, and if necessary treat, all sheep brought in before allowing them to mix with the flock.

Orf on a finger

Orf (Contagious Pustular Dermatisis)

Orf is a very painful condition affecting sheep of all ages. It is caused by a virus which enters the skin through minor cuts and abrasions, and it can also affect humans who come into contact with

125

An extreme case of orf

infected sheep, causing painful, scabby areas on the hands, wrists, inner arms and face. For this reason it is necessary to wear protective gloves at all times when dealing with this disease.

Having penetrated the skin, the virus multiplies rapidly, causing small spots which suppurate and join together to form grape-like clusters. It is confined to the non-woolly areas in both ewes and lambs. In lactating ewes, the udders and teats become infected, and in young lambs it affects the lips, gums and nose, resulting in the doubly distressing situation where hungry lambs with painful mouths are prevented from feeding because of the soreness and pain in the ewes' teats. The condition clears up in a few weeks and healing occurs. Orf can also affect older weaned lambs in the autumn and the genital areas of ewes and rams, making the rams very reluctant to work. The condition known as strawberry footrot which causes raw red bleeding areas on the non-woolly areas of the faces and legs is believed to be related to the orf virus.

Being a virus, orf does not respond to antibiotics and is virtually impossible to cure. Secondary infections of the lesions can be guarded against by the use of an antibiotic spray.

It is possible to vaccinate against orf. The vaccine is applied to an area of bare skin, preferably between a foreleg and the chest wall. Do not use disinfectant or spirit to clean the skin before applying the vaccine, which is a modified form of the living virus, as this would destroy it before it can produce the desired effect. The skin must be lightly scratched where the vaccine is applied, and later a scab will form.

The disease is most troublesome in lactating ewes with new-born lambs, and flocks in which orf has occurred previously should be vaccinated two months before protection is required. On no account should sheep in flocks where the disease has never occurred be vaccinated. This is because the mild infection introduced by the modified living virus produces scabs at the site of the vaccination and these, as they fall from the sheep, are liable to affect any 'clean' sheep bought in.

An outbreak of orf can be controlled to a certain extent, especially in young suckling lambs, by vaccinating non-affected members of the flock. Seek the advice of your vet if an outbreak occurs, and follow the manufacturer's instructions carefully when using the vaccine.

Lameness

Lameness can occur in a number of different ways. Watch the sheep to see how it moves and which is the lame leg or legs. Catch the sheep, immobilise it and examine each foot in turn.

One of the commonest forms of lameness is caused by vegetable matter and mud becoming impacted between the hooves, and by mud becoming trapped in the layer of horn on the hoof wall of overgrown feet. Once this is removed and the hoof pared, the sheep will quickly become sound.

Look for a reddened and moist area between the digits and also for abscesses around the top of the hoof. If these are not found, feel the leg for any hot spots or swelling which might indicate a sprain or hairline fracture. Check that there are no dislocated joints.

Footrot and Scald

Footrot is a very painful and debilitating disease if allowed to go untreated and is directly responsible for causing huge financial losses to the sheep industry every year. While it is not a killer disease in itself, it can severely affect the performance of all classes of sheep from young lambs and ewes to rams, the latter especially at mating time.

It is caused by the joint action of several types of organisms, one of which is quite common in some areas of the UK. It causes scald – an inflammation of the skin between the two digits of the foot – and it can occur in all classes of sheep at any time of the year, but is more commonly seen when the sheep, particularly lambs, are grazing long, lush grass in the spring, and also shortly after ewes have been housed on straw bedding in the winter. The particular organism which causes scald can only live for three weeks away from the sheep, and careful use of a footbath can eradicate it from the flock, especially if clean land is available for

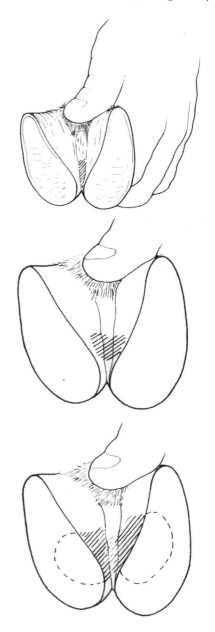

Hatched areas show the spread of footrot

grazing after footbathing.

True footrot occurs when a second organism invades the inflamed tissue between the digits. This causes an under-running of the sole of the foot, and eventually the horny outer wall, reaching right up to the toe. If this under-run tissue is lifted or pared off, the exposed area resembles the gills of a mushroom, except that it is usually dark grey in colour, and has a characteristic pungent, unpleasant smell. Treatment consists of paring away all the under-run horn from the sole and outer surface of the digit. The bulk of the material can be cut away with straight-bladed secateurs, but a very sharp knife should be used for the more precise trimming necessary to expose the fullest extent of the infection. The dividing line between healthy and infected tissue is a very fine one, and every care should be taken to avoid the bleeding which will occur if the healthy tissue is cut, especially in the region of the toe.

Here it should be stated that if footrot is treated as soon as a sheep is seen to be walking lame, a lot of pain for the sheep and a lot of work for the shepherd can be avoided. An antibiotic spray can be used to treat the infection, and the sheep should be stood on a hard surface while the foot dries.

When footrot or scald is present, it is much easier to control if all the sheep can be stood in a shallow bath of 10 percent zinc sulphate solution for up to an hour. This long period enables the solution to penetrate pockets where the causal organisms might have been missed when paring. The feet should then be allowed to dry before returning to pasture. Formalin is also used for treatment and control, but it has a number of disadvantages. The fumes given off are toxic, and it is ineffective when the footbath becomes contaminated with dung or soil. It makes the hoof very hard and is very painful if used on feet where footrot has already been exposed. The feet should be soaked for a much shorter time with formalin solution, about two minutes usually being sufficient.

Both zinc sulphate and formalin are difficult to dispose of and both are poisonous to fish if allowed into streams, ponds or ditches. Zinc sulphate may be used and reused as it does not deteriorate in contact with vegetable matter.

When treating footrot it is important that all foot parings are collected and burnt and that all tools are disinfected by immersing them in 10 prcent zinc sulphate solution between each sheep.

In severe cases of footrot, and particularly with valuable rams, consult a veterinary surgeon about the possibility of an antibiotic injection as treatment after paring. Prevention can be assisted by using a footrot vaccine. Two vaccinations are required initially, followed by two booster injections each year. The vaccine is expensive to buy and any partly used bottles must be discarded which adds to the expense for small flock owners.

Foot Abscesses

These can cause very painful lameness, occurring where the horn of the hoof joins the skin of the coronet. Consult your veterinary surgeon.

Granulomas or Proudflesh

When the feet are allowed to become badly overgrown, the horn may aggravate the soft tissue between the digits, or the under-run sole may rub against the sensitive layer below it and cause excessive growth with associated bleeding, especially from the area of the toe. This is a very painful condition and in the spring and summer may attract the blowfly to lay its eggs in the foot. (This is also the case with ordinary footrot).

Granulomas need to be surgically removed by a vet and even so they take a long time to heal.

Roundworms

All sheep carry some worms but it is the balance between numbers and the state of the sheep's resistance which determines whether disease develops. Pasture management is an important factor in controlling roundworm population. The old saying 'A sheep's worst enemy is another sheep' indicates that heavy stocking rates, coupled with infrequent moves onto clean pasture, can result in heavy infestation, with a resultant loss in condition and a reduced growth rate.

Roundworms occur in a variety of forms. Those that cause problems for sheep start life as eggs passed out with the faeces onto the pasture. Given suitable climatic conditions of warmth and moisture, the eggs develop into larvae which go through several stages before migrating onto grass stems where they are eaten by sheep. Two weeks later they are mature adults, mating and producing eggs.

This is an oversimplification of the matter because different types of roundworm prefer different parts of the digestive tract in which to live and produce eggs. Some can lie dormant in the gut until favourable conditions for further development come along. When this happens, a rapid explosion of activity occurs. Some types hibernate through the winter as larval stages on the pasture and only when the temperature rises in the spring (which also stimulates the growth of new grass) do they hatch in massive numbers to be eaten by young lambs and cause a lot of problems.

Diarrhoea, dehydration and reduced appetite are symptoms which can indicate worm infestation, although these can be confused with symptoms of other conditions. Even with moderate or light infestations there will be a reduced growth rate in the lambs and the fleeces will appear to be dull, dry and lacking in bloom.

Anthelmintics are drugs that control internal parasites and a wide range of them is available for the control of roundworms. For the treatment to be effective, it is very important to follow the manufacturer's instructions carefully to match the dosage required to the weight of the animal being treated. There is evidence that some types of roundworm are becoming resistant to some of the drugs being used. Check with your vet as to the most suitable anthelmintic if your sheep have a particular problem.

Clean pasture is invaluable in providing an efficient management aid in that newly dosed sheep can graze without the challenge of immediate re-infestation. Similarly, mixed grazing with cattle can do a lot to reduce the uptake of worm larvae.

Tapeworms

Tapeworms are flat, ribbon-like parasites which live in the small intestine of the sheep. The worm consists of a tiny head which attaches itself to the wall of the gut, either by a sucker or with hooks, and it feeds in that position. The ribbon-like body consists of a series of segments which are grown from the head and which may reach several metres in length. They are in fact packets of eggs which are shed from the end of the worm and pass out with the faeces. They require an intermediate host for their further development, and can be easily seen as flat, white, short pieces of tape. Although unsightly, they rarely cause any great harm to the sheep, unless present in large numbers.

Many anthelmintics used to control roundworms are also effective with tapeworms. Details will be found on the manufacturer's package.

Gid

There are a number of different kinds of tapeworm, and this disease of the central nervous system is caused when sheep eat grass contaminated by the larval stage of a tapeworm found in dogs. Over a period of time the larvae migrate through the bloodstream and begin developing when they reach the nervous tissue, including the brain. Here they grow into a cyst filled with fluid containing tapeworm heads.

The symptoms which may indicate gid can vary, and are easily confused with other nervous diseases. Sometimes the affected sheep will lie with the head turned to one side, or hold it abnormally high. Others will walk in circles, always turning the same way, and all will eventually go down, become comatose and die. The time taken for this to happen varies considerably, and if the veterinary surgeon is called in early and diagnoses gid, the chances are that he will be able to operate successfully and remove the cyst.

If the uncooked head of a dead sheep suffering from

gid is eaten by a dog, the tapeworm heads develop into adult tapeworms and the life cycle of the parasite begins again. It is possible to break this cycle by ensuring that any sheep offal fed to dogs is boiled for at least one hour. All dogs owned should be dosed with a medication obtainable from your vet, which is capable of killing all of these tapeworms, including the heads. This should be done every two months, but of course it will not prevent other dogs and foxes coming onto the property and contaminating the grassland.

Hydatid Disease

There is another type of tapeworm, less than a centimetre in length, which lives in the small intestine of the dog. The ripe segments from these tiny tapeworms are passed out in the faeces of the dog, some adhering to the hairy coat. Infection of the sheep occurs when the grazing animal eats grass contaminated by infected dogs. Humans, especially children, can become infected by stroking and cuddling dogs and then accidentally swallowing the tapeworm eggs.

The hydatid cyst will grow in any part of the body, but commonly in the lungs and liver. Human beings cannot become infected by eating lamb or mutton. Prevention by strict hygiene when handling dogs and by regularly dosing them with an anthelmintic against this particular tapeworm, called Echinococcus granulosus, is desirable. Never feed raw sheep meat to dogs – it should be cooked for at least an hour – and dispose of any carcases so that they cannot be scavenged by dogs or foxes. Discuss prevention with your vet.

Liver Fluke

The fluke is a flat, leaf-like parasite which is common in wet, marshy areas. It requires an intermediate host, a mud snail, for its development. For the sheep, the problem starts when it eats grass which is carrying the encysted stage of the fluke. On reaching the sheep's gut, the immature fluke makes its way through the gut wall and searches out the liver. Once in the liver it feeds voraciously, and on becoming adult it anchors itself in the bile duct and takes blood from the wall. It lays eggs which pass out with the faeces. These then hatch and seek out a mud snail, in which they multiply, thereafter leaving the snail and encysting themselves on grass to begin the cycle again.

Affected sheep become very anaemic and lose condition. A watery swelling appears under the lower jaw and the membranes of the eyes and mouth become very pale.

If the presence of fluke is suspected, take a dung sample to your vet who will be able to tell you whether fluke eggs are present. The vet will also advise on the method of treatment most pertinent to the condition of your sheep. Cattle, goats, deer and rabbits can also act as hosts and carriers of fluke.

Pulpy Kidney and Other Causes of Sudden Death

There is a group of diseases (including tetanus) caused by Clostridium bacteria which can cause sudden death, and it is very nearly always the best sheep which are affected. Fortunately there are very good vaccines available which will give complete protection from specific diseases if given routinely and according to the manufacturer's instructions. It is recommended that for all breeding stock a '7 in 1' type vaccine is used. If well grown and sold for slaughter before 16 weeks of age, lambs born in a vaccinated flock will not normally need vaccination, as the protection given by antibodies in the ewe's colostrum will be sufficient. Other vaccines giving protection against fewer clostridial diseases are available.

It should always be assumed that any bought-in sheep are unvaccinated. They should be given a full dose of vaccine immediately, followed by a booster dose four weeks later. Another booster dose for the ewes four weeks before lambing commences ensures that newborn lambs are protected, provided they get an adequate supply of colostrum. If lambing is protracted it may be necessary to give a further booster dose of vaccine to late-lambing ewes.

Home-bred ewe lambs born to vaccinated ewes and intended as flock replacements will require a primary vaccination at two to three months of age, followed by a secondary dose four to six weeks later. If they are bred from in their first year they, like the ewes, will require a booster dose four weeks before lambing. Similarly, ram lambs kept for breeding should be treated like the ewe lambs, but in subsequent years a booster dose around four weeks before mating commences will suffice.

This vaccine should be given subcutaneously at a site high on the neck of the sheep. Occasionally an abscess or small nodule will form at the injection site and if this is on the neck, it will not reduce the value of the skin after slaughter.

Pneumonia

The bacteria which cause pneumonia in sheep come in many different types. Deaths from pneumonia can occur in all classes of sheep and at any time of the year. Often the first sign of the disease is a dead sheep, or a short period of laboured breathing and frothing at the mouth followed by death. Other forms of the disease can be treated with long-acting antibiotics if detected early.

Pasteurellosis (pneumonia) is a very complex and variable condition. Periods of stress, which can include bad weather, can predispose a flock to infection, and if the level of stress is great enough outbreaks can occur even though the sheep have been vaccinated.

A post-mortem examination of sheep which die from pneumonia will reveal plum-coloured lungs surrounded by bloodstained fluid, and in many cases death will have occurred so rapidly that it is impossible to observe any symptoms.

It is possible to vaccinate against certain types of pasteurella, and to be effective the vaccine must be appropriate to the particular requirements of the flock as determined by laboratory tests. It is possible to buy a combined clostridial and pasteurella vaccine, but little, if any, immunity to pasteurella is passed to the lambs in the antibodies contained in the colostrum, compared to the cover given against the clostridial diseases. If early protection is required for the lambs, they must be given pasteurella-only vaccine when two weeks old if they are born to ewes which have previously been vaccinated.

Lambs born to ewes which have not been vaccinated can be given pasteurella-only vaccine at birth, followed two weeks later by a second injection. Ewe lambs retained for breeding will require one annual booster injection.

Metabolic Diseases

Metabolic diseases associated with feeding and production are sudden in onset and can lead to death in a very short time. They arise as a consequence of food intake not meeting urgent requirements.

Pregnancy Toxaemia

Also known as twin lamb disease, this occurs during

the last month of pregnancy, most commonly in ewes that are carrying two or three lambs. At this time the unborn lambs are making heavy nutritional demands on the ewe. Pregnancy toxaemia can affect both thin and fat ewes and is usually caused by an insufficient uptake of nutritious food.

Concentrates should be fed during the last six weeks of pregnancy, starting with 100g per day, increasing weekly to reach 750g per day by lambing. The protein content of the concentrates should be 17 percent, and it is helpful if the merchant supplying the feed gives you a list of the ingredients so that the stated analysis can be checked.

Ewes affected by pregnancy toxaemia get separated from the rest of the flock, refuse food and become blind. After a few days they are unable to stand and they assume unnatural positional behaviour. Front legs may be stretched out in front and the head pressed down into the ground. Symptoms include twitching and trembling of the lips and ears, and grinding teeth. If the ewe is left untreated, death follows fairly quickly. The advice of the vet should be quickly sought if pregnancy toxaemia is suspected, and the ewe moved to warm, comfortable conditions under cover.

Prevention of this disease is easier if sheep are housed, as a more careful check can be kept on their condition. The target condition score at lambing is 3.5, and thin ewes and shy feeders which are often bullied at the trough should be separated and given extra concentrates. Ewes which are lame or have teeth problems are also at risk, as are ewes kept outside in periods of very bad weather. See that all the ewes have sufficient trough space. It is helpful to be able to put all the feed in the troughs before allowing the sheep access to it, perhaps in a separate enclosure or an adjoining field. This will allow fair shares for all.

The bulk part of the diet should be of good quality hay, and the concentrate fed first. A stomach full of poor quality food is of no use to a ewe carrying three lambs. Four-fifths of the eventual birthweight is gained during the last two months of pregnancy.

Overfat ewes too are at risk, simply because internal layers of fat restrict the space available for any increase in nutritious food required to feed the unborn lambs.

Death is caused by a breakdown of the metabolism and a lowering of blood sugar levels. One school of thought suggests that if the ewe is shorn the metabolism is stirred into action again by the demands of the ewe she attempts to convert energy into warmth!

It is best to prevent the disease by careful management of the flock, particularly in the later stages of pregnancy, as the recovery rate is very low.

Hypocalcaemia

This disease can occur during late pregnancy or early lactation, and it is caused by a low level of calcium in the blood. Listlessness and depression precede loss of consciousness, but a subcutaneous injection of 100ml of 20 percent calcium borogluconate will effect a rapid return to normal. Divide the dose and inject at five or six different sites on the body.

Hypomagnesaemia

The onset of this disease can be extremely rapid and usually occurs when newly lambed ewes are turned out onto very lush grass. It is caused be low levels of magnesium in the blood, and is characterised by a stiffness when walking, and twitching and spasms, followed by convulsions and death. Prompt treatment, consisting of a subcutaneous injection of 100ml of magnesium-fortified 20 percent calcium borogluconate, divided and injected at several sites as with hypocalcaemia, is necessary.

The main problem in treating this disease is the speed at which it develops, and unless the person in charge is present and very observant, quite often the only indication is a dead sheep. Prevention can be assisted by offering a mineral mixture containing calcined magnesite, but as this is an unpalatable ingredient it needs to be disguised to make it acceptable by adding some molasses or treacle. It is possible to buy compound feeds containing calcined magnesite, and these should be introduced into the rations gradually just before lambing, and continued for a few weeks afterwards while animals are at risk.

Heavy dressings of nitrogenous fertilisers encourage a rapid growth of young grass in the spring which also reduces the uptake of both calcium and magnesium, a point to be borne in mind when considering how best to manage the available grassland.

Diseases Associated with Lambing

Abortion

There are a number of different organisms which can cause abortion in sheep. Abortion can also be caused by other factors such as worrying dogs, malnutrition, incorrect handling and being forced too quickly through narrow gateways, to name but a few. In some cases of abortion early or midway through pregnancy the foetus may be so small that it passes unnoticed by the shepherd. A single ewe aborting may give no cause for alarm and be dismissed as one of the accepted risks of keeping livestock.

When a number of abortions occur, producing dead or very weakly foetuses, the vet should be called in without delay as it is only by microscopic bacteriological examination of aborted material that an accurate diagnosis can be made, and, if appropriate, the type of vaccine required to minimise further losses be recommended.

Domestic cats are responsible for spreading infection

causing one type of abortion in sheep, which is also contagious to humans. Consequently, extreme care should be taken when handling and disposing of any aborted material, and pregnant women should stay away from ewes at lambing time.

Mastitis

Mastitis can be present in the ewe flock in both chronic and acute forms. The chronic form is usually discovered when the ewes are being inspected prior to selection for the breeding flock. It is identifiable as a fibrous lump or series of lumps in the udder. If the ewe is used for breeding, the affected side of the udder will not produce any milk. It is not known when infection occurs and there is no known cure. Affected ewes should be culled.

The acute form commonly occurs early in lactation. Affected ewes are clearly ill and appear to be walking stiffly, and the udder is swollen and grows increasingly cold to the touch. The udder rapidly becomes inflamed, turning red or purplish-blue and eventually black. If the teat is drawn, a bloodstained fluid comes away. The inflammation may extend along the belly of the ewe if she survives and eventually all the dead coloured tissue will fall off leaving a raw, bleeding surface. Healing takes a long time and the exposed tissue is vulnerable to fly strike. Consult the vet as to the best course of action. There is no effective treatment for this condition, and if the ewe survives she should be culled.

Masititis

Navel Infections

The umbilical cord of a newborn lamb is moist and immediately after birth it is in contact with many different types of bacteria on the ground. This is the route by which certain harmful organisms gain entry to the body of the lamb. It is comparatively easy to prevent this from happening by applying an antiseptic dressing to the navel as soon as the lamb is born and then placing the lamb on a bed of clean straw. The aim is to dry up the cord as quickly as possible and to disinfect the area of the body around it.

Several preparations are suitable for use as a dressing:

- Tincture of iodine
- Antibiotic aerosol

- A weak solution of copper sulphate

A dressing which can be contained in a wide-necked bottle is preferable to an aerosol as the wet cord and the area immediately surrounding it can be totally immersed in the liquid. Hold the lamb vertically by its forelegs and put the navel cord into the neck of the bottle. Lift the bottle at a right angle to the lamb and press it gently into the belly.

Coccidiosis

Coccidiosis is a disease of young lambs. Older sheep will have developed an immunity through previous contact with the parasite, but they can still pass on the infection. The disease occurs mostly in housed flocks, although it can also infect lambs on heavily stocked pasture through contaminated faeces.

Infected lambs become unthrifty with a loss of appetite and develop a mild diarrhoea which causes dehydration. If coccidiosis is suspected, consult your vet over treatment and preventative measures to be taken in subsequent years.

Notifiable Diseases

Zoonoses

Animal diseases which are communicable to human beings are called zoonoses, and while some may cause only slight problems, others can be dangerous and even life-threatening. Anyone who is working with sheep or in contact with them when a zoonotic disease is present or suspected should seek medical advice without delay if they feel unwell.

The following are zoonoses:

- Anthrax
- Rabies
- Salmonellosis
- Hydatid Disease
- Orf
- Brucellosis
- Chlamydiosis
- Listeriosis
- Toxoplamosis
- All Abortion Agents

The last five on this list all pose a threat to pregnant women, as they can cause abortion or serious defects if in contact with the unborn foetus. Pregnant women should keep away from sheep at lambing time.

Your Veterinary Surgeon

Some veterinary surgeons are more involved in sheep than others, so try to find and get to know one with whom you can readily communicate. Also, do this before you encounter an emergency. It will cost you money, but a general advisory visit to discuss management, feeding, a vaccination programme, a worming policy, etc., could prove to be a good investment.

Don't forget that you can take a sheep which is in trouble to the surgery and save yourself a call-out fee.

Chapter Nine
Keeping Records

All flock owners will find it extremely useful to keep a record of day-to-day events with the flock. The records can contain as little or as much of the history of the flock as the owner decides, and can include details relating to individual sheep, food purchased, grassland management, veterinary treatment, etc. Records of the performance of individual sheep start with accurate identification. Contact your local Animal Health Divisional Office or DEFRA to keep up to date with your legal requirements.

Identification

Each sheep in the flock should carry a permanent mark

which will identify it and distinguish it from its flockmates in all the various forms of recording. In addition to an individual number, the mark can also indicate the year of birth and in some cases the sire.

All sheep in the flock must now carry a permanent ear tag which will identify and distinguish the individual sheep from the rest of the flock in relation to the various means of keeping records. The new EU rules for sheep identification came in force in July 2005.

Ear Tag

Ear tags

Ear tags are supplied in various shapes, sizes and colours and are available in both plastic and metal. Some metal tags are tamperproof and cannot be removed easily. The manufacturer's instructions should always be followed if you are using these tags on young lambs, remembering that the ears will grow and therefore require more space within the tag. Special pliers are required for their application.

Types of Ear tag

The UK tag includes the following information:

- A special flock number (UK plus six numbers).
- The sheep's individual identification number

This tag is attached to the sheep on the holding of their birth (the farm on which they were born).

Baseline 'S' tag

- A special flock mark (S plus six numbers)
- The sheep's individual identification number

This tag is used for identifying sheep not on their holding of birth and which do not already carry a UK tag.

Movement 'S' tag

- A flock mark (S plus six numbers)

This tag is applied in addition to the UK tag and is used for identifying sheep moving off a holding which is not their holding of birth. This also applies to moves to the slaughterer and to temporary or common grazing. Temporary marks are no longer legal.

You do not need to apply a Movement S tag if:

*   You record the animals full identification number in the flock register and on the AMLI movement document.
*   You are moving animals to a show or exhibition
*   The animal has a tag with the flock or herd mark of the current holding it is moving from
*   The animal is return to its home holding from temporary grazing land or from shearing and dipping
*   The animal is moving to or from the vets

Replacement R tag

*   A UK flock mark
*   The sheep's individual identification number

This tag must be red and is used to replace a lost UK, a basline S or a previous R tag.

All sheep born after July 2005 must wear a UK tag within six monts of birth and before the animal moves from it's holding of birth.

Additional guidance can be obtained form your local Animal Health Office or DEFRA.

Tattoo

Tattoos

As all sheep must now be identified with an ear tag tattoos are no longer acceptable as an official method of identification. They may however be a useful addition in your own sheep management. They are easier to read in the ears of white-faced sheep as they show up clearly when black tattooing ink is used. For sheep with coloured faces white or green tattooing ink is more suitable, but in all cases it is essential that the mark is placed centrally in the ear, between the two main sinews. With some pedigree breeds one ear is reserved for the flock number and the official registered mark of the breed society, while the other is left for the use of the flock owner.

Ear notching

Ear notching

As all sheep must now be identified with an ear tag ear notching is no longer acceptable as an official method of identification. However it is still used as a method of identification. Ear notching using special pliers can be done at any age. It does not, however, indicate the year of birth, and for this a single letter tattooed in the ear is needed. The sheep's left ear is used for units and the right ear for tens. Five positions on the left ear will give sufficient spaces from one to nine, and from ten to ninety on the right. Sheep number seventy-nine would require notches denoting fifty and twenty on the right ear and five and four on the left, with a tattooed letter in the right ear indicating the year of birth.

Systems of Recording

Once there is a system of identification, which is essential in pedigree flocks, records can be kept of the health and performance of the sheep.

Some breed societies have designed a pro-forma with headings under which details can be entered as they occur, and from which an accurate assessment can be made of the performance of the flock from year to year.

A loose-leaf system, based on one page for each sheep can, for example, include details of the breed, the ear number, the age and a record of the sire and dam. In the case of a ewe, details of mating, the ram used, the date of service, together with the date of lambing and the sex and birth weight of the lambs born, any subsequent weighings, how disposed of and the price obtained can be recorded on a form.

For a ram, in addition to individual details, the number of ewes served, the total of lambs born to them, alive and dead, together with details of the total sum realised when the lambs are sold, will allow a comparison to be made between the performance of the rams used, and between the performance of the same ram in different years.

In addition to the performance of individuals within the flock, a record of the sheep food purchased and times in the year when feeding was considered necessary, can be recorded. Any cultivations required by grazing land and fertiliser applied, together with capital costs incurred for housing, fencing and equipment may provide interesting (or frightening!) information and can be used in calculating a profit and loss account.

Medicine Records

A separate record of all medicines purchased and dates administered is now a legal requirement with the following information needing to be recorded:

- The name of the product
- The date of purchase
- The quantity purchased
- The withdrawal period
- The name and address of the supplier

At the time when the medicine is given the owner must record:

- The name of the product
- The date of administration
- The quantity given
- The name and address of the supplier

A record of the means and whereabouts of the disposal must also be noted. Additionally records of all of these details must be kept for five years. Detailed information on Veterinary Medicines Regulations can be obtained from your local Animal Health Divisional Office.

Disposal of Carcases

Dead sheep or fallen stock can no longer be buried or burnt in the open. This is because of the risk of disease through air pollution or through the pollution of the water courses and groundwater.

The animal must now be collected, transported and disposed of at an approved knacker or hunt kennel or incinerated or dealt with under the National Fallen Stock Scheme. To obtain details of approved permises contact DEFRA.

Registration

It is now compulsory for anyone keeping sheep to register with their local Animal Health Office. An individual flock number can then be issued and aholding number obtained from DEFRA.

Movement

All movements of sheep to and from your holding must be recorded within three days of the movement taking place. Specific movement documents must be obtained, completed and returned to your local Animal Health Office. These forms must contain the following:

- The holding number
- The name of the owner/keeper
- Details of the sheep
- Transportation information
- Loading, departure and unloading times
- Destination details

There are specific rules on the transportation of animals over a certain distance and for movement out of Britain.

Records of all movements must be kept for inspection by the Animal Health Officer who may choose to visit the premises.

Keeping Individual Records

It is also a requirement to keep indiviual sheep records. These should include the follwing:

- The total number of sheep within the flock
- The details of the sheep that have been moved from the property
- Sheep losses and their causes
- Breding information

Transport

There are occasions when it is necessary to transport members of the flock. It might be to a show, to a market or fair or to a shearing centre. There is a statutory obligation under the Animal Health Act 1981 and the Welfare of Animals Transport Order 1997 as amended for certain legal requirements to be observed when transporting stock.

The main ones apply to all forms of transport and may be summarised under the following headings.

The roof must be weatherproof.

Ventilation should be adequate and appropriate to the number of stock being transported.

The interior of the transport vehicle should be free from projections likely to cause injury or suffering.

The floor should be of non-slip design and/or strewn with straw or similar material to provide a proper foothold.
Ramps should be designed to prevent slipping and have no gap between the ramp and the floor of the transport vehicle in which a foot or leg can be trapped.

Sidegates should be of sufficient height and strength to avoid falls from the ramp.

Partitions/dividers should be fitted if the floor exceeds 3.1m in length. If a full load is not carried, the pens will need to be smaller.

Chapter Ten
The Shepherd's Calendar

In keeping and caring for sheep in flocks both large or small, there follows a sequence of events throughout the year. It is the same for both early-and late-lambing flocks and begins in late summer or early autumn with the selection of breeding stock. The future crop of lambs will depend to a certain extent on daily observations by the shepherd of the prevailing conditions. The state of the grazing, the weather, supplementary food and preventive medicine all need to be assessed constantly and adjusted as necessary.

July, August, September

Make a thorough inspection of the ewe flock, paying particular attention to teeth, feet and udders. Mark for culling any that do not meet basic requirements, segregate them and sell them for meat.

If additional sheep are required, buy the best that can be afforded.

October

Get the ewes onto a rising plane of nutrition by putting them onto clean, fresh grazing or by feeding a small amount (100g) of concentrates each morning. Aim for a condition score of 3.5 at mating.

Fit the ram's harness in position a few days before mating is to begin and tighten if necessary when adding the coloured crayon.

Introduce the ram five months before the planned date for lambing, and record the date on which each ewe is served. The average gestation period is 147 days.

November

Stop feeding concentrate to the ewes when they have been mated, but feed hay if the quality and quantity of the grazing deteriorates. The hay must be of good quality, free from mould, and sweet-smelling. It should be fed from covered hayracks as sheep will not eat wet hay.

December, January, February

Consider housing the ewes if the weather is bad, using barley straw for bedding. Continue feeding hay ad lib. Introduce concentrates six weeks before lambing is due to begin. Vaccinate each ewe with a booster dose of vaccine against clostridial diseases immediately before lambing.

Prepare the lambing kit and ensure that all records are up to date.

March, April

Lambing. Record lamb dates of birth and birth weights. Carry out tailing and castrating.

Continue feeding ewes, adding succulent foods such as roots, cabbage type green food or soaked sugar beet pulp if possible.

Creep feed lambs.

Give ewes a dose of broad spectrum anthelmintics and trim feet. Weather permitting, turn ewes and lambs out onto clean grazing by day, returning to a communal pen in the sheep house at night. After a period of hardening off they can be left out overnight.

Dose lambs against worms at six weeks of age and

thereafter at monthly intervals.

May, June

Reduce the concentrate feeding for the ewes as the quantity and quality of the grazing increases. Offer hay in covered hayracks if there is any scouring.

Carry out crutching, shearing and dipping against fly strike.

July

Wean lambs onto fresh, clean grazing. Sell lambs destined for the meat market as they reach the optimum weight.

Vaccinate any remaining lambs against clostridial diseases as they reach sixteen weeks of age.

August, September

Attend store lamb, breeding ewe and ram sales. Make up the breeding flock.

Chapter Eleven
Showing Sheep

Many small flock owners get pleasure from taking their sheep to shows and competing for the honour of winning prize cards and rosettes. Many local shows now have classes for all types of sheep and lambs, and as they are usually held at weekends it means that more people can spare the time to attend.

All sheep shown, whether pure or crossbred, should have good conformation and be well-grown for their age. Depending on the breed, they should be in good condition, with the down breeds having a condition score of at least 3.5 or 4. The fleece should be clean, the feet well trimmed and it is a great help for both sheep and shepherd if the sheep is taught to walk on a halter.

Halter trained sheep are able to show themselves off to the judge without involving the handler in a rodeo routine!

Selection

When selecting a sheep for show, start looking well before the date of the show and select an animal that has the indefinable quality of 'character.' This is the sheep that is always appealing to the eye in any position and one that always stands out from its flock-mates. If it is a purebred or pedigree sheep, check the list of points which have been drawn up by the breed society concerned as being particularly desirable. Match the selected sheep as nearly as possible to that list. Select a sheep with a bold eye and an alert expression, a straight back and standing four square on straight legs. Observe the way it moves when walking towards and away from you, especially when being led on a halter.

Halter Training

Some show judges ask for an entry to be turned loose in the show ring so that they can see for themselves how the sheep moves naturally, but others ask for it to be paraded on a halter. Use a cotton halter for training rather than one made from polypropylene and fit a piece of rubber tubing to the part of the halter which goes under the lower jaw. This will prevent the halter from becoming too tight if the sheep puts up a lot of resistance, and thus

A sheep halter

prevent chafing the skin which might lead to an unsightly scar. Have a long lead rope on the halter when beginning the training and walk behind the sheep in such a way that it can be restrained if it tries to break away. A push from behind will usually encourage it to walk forward. After a half-hour session each day for a few days, it will quickly become accustomed to the halter and the handler, and walk beside him in a natural way.

167

The next step is to get the animal to stand still while on the halter and to stand in a way in which it shows itself off to the best advantage. It may be necessary to move a leg slightly to achieve the best position. This can be done either by gently pushing or pulling the sheep to one side or the other, or by moving it with the hand.

Showmanship

Wear a clean white coat and keep the sheep in a correct position all the time that it is before the judge. It should not be allowed to graze or turn around or lie down. Onlookers might be amused to see this, but it could cost a prize if it happened just when the judge looked back in order to make a comparison with another sheep. Keep the head of the sheep at a naturally comfortable height while it is being held, neither too high nor too low. Stand in front of the sheep while the judge is standing behind the line-up, but move to one side so that he can see the front when he comes around to the other side. Watch the judge as well as the sheep all the time and try to convince him by showmanship and without words that you have the best sheep!

Dressing

The fleeces carried by the various breeds of sheep vary a great deal between the fine, short staple of the Southdown and the long, coarse wool of the Scottish Blackface. Others like the Wensleydale have long, lustrous fleeces which hang in ringlets, and the Herdwick and Welsh Mountain contain a high proportion of kemp in their wool.

Different types of wool require different treatments before being presented for the judge's inspection. Tradition dictates that on some breeds unnatural shapes are created, using hand shears, while others have a minimum of trimming with a programme of dipping in a variety of dips. In all cases, the fleece should be clean and free from dung and vegetable matter.

Any washing that is required should be done about ten days before the show. Tie up the sheep and soak with water from a hosepipe or buckets. Use soap flakes and work up a lather in the wool, using the fingers to tease out any matted locks. If a swimbath is available, fill it with clean water and allow the sheep to swim in it to rinse out the soap and dirt. Keep the sheep on a halter while swimming, as fat sheep with heavy fleeces can be at risk in the bath. Use the halter to pull the sheep to the ramp leading out of the bath if the animal appears to be distressed in any way. If no swimbath is available for rinsing, use a hosepipe or bucket with plenty of clean water.

Choose a dry day for the washing as it is important that the sheep dries quickly. Never put the sheep under cover while still wet. Washing with soap will leave the fleece soft, white and open in texture, and it will respond to being dipped in a bath containing show dip. These dips are designed specifically to firm up the wool in shortwools and to add to the lustre and purl effect in longwools. They also take away the flat whiteness which is apparent after washing in soap.

As each breed of sheep has its own traditional shape or appearance when brought out for show, it is not proposed here to go into the requirements for each breed. Suffice it to say that if the plan is to produce show entries trimmed with hand shears, then take a course by an expert on how it should be done. The equipment required – hand shears, sharpening stone, carding wire on heavy wooden backs, halters and an old shearing comb for cleaning the carding wire – is modest, but the skill in using it is not!

Take consolation from the fact that a good sheep is attractive to the experienced eye whether it is trimmed or not.

Lambs can be shown in their natural fleece, while older sheep will look better if they are carrying about four months' growth of wool. All that is required on a sheep that has been docked is that the wool on the end of the tail is squared off parallel to the ground.

The Texel breed has stipulated that all its show animals must be shown in a natural condition. Any trimming or shaping is not allowed, although faces and legs can be washed clean.

Fleece Wool

A less demanding type of showing is in classes for shorn fleeces. Select the fleeces while they are still on the sheep and swim the sheep in clean water without soap, dip or disinfectant added, around four weeks before shearing. Ask the shearer to take special care when shearing and wrap the shorn fleece according to the instructions in the show schedule. Place the fleece in a large paper sack as this will help to retain its wrapped shape. Avoid plastic sacks which will cause the wool to sweat. Identify your fleeces with a clean well-written label.

Showing Butcher's Lambs

To show lambs in the butcher's lamb class requires a knowledge of carcase classification. This is a way by which the conformation and degree of fatness is described by visual appraisal, and given a code by the Meat and Livestock Commission staff working in the abattoir. The conformation classification is graded on the scale E,U,R,O,P with E being the best and P the poorest. The fatness is assessed by handling the tail and the spinous and transverse processes of the loin and grading between 1 (the leanest) and 5 (the fattest).

The preferred weight of the carcase is between fifteen and twenty kilograms, so the aim is for a finished carcase grading of 2 or 3 in the conformation class E or U. Grades 3, 4 and 5 are further subdivided into L and H, with L denoting low fat cover and H denoting high. The preferred classification by most meat buyers is within the range of 2 and 3L. The weight of the carcase will be around 45 percent of the liveweight of the lamb, depending on the degree of fatness.

Great care should be taken at all times with loading and transporting lambs, but particularly if the lamb is to be shown as a carcase. It should never be held or picked up by the wool as this will cause distress to the lamb and result in unsightly bruising of the carcase. Avoid any sharp projections which could cause injury in the transport used to take the lambs to the show, and also avoid abscesses on the carcase caused by faulty injection techniques. Injection sites should be high up on the neck and the hypodermic needles used should be sharp and sterile.

Rolling a shortwool fleece

Step 1. Place the flesh side of the fleece down and fold flank towards the centre.

Step 2. Do the same with the other side.

Step 3. Turn the britch end and roll firmly towards the neck.

Step 4. After folding, part the fleece.

Step 5. Without twisting, tuck the neck wool firmly into the body of the fleece.

Step 6. The resulting fleece is firm and secure

Chapter Twelve
Grassland Management

The flock owner with only a small area of land on which to graze the sheep will perhaps find it difficult to do very much in the way of constructive management to bring about improvement in the grass. Nitrogenous fertiliser used in the early springtime will give a boost to the growth of grass but it must be balanced by adding phosphate and potash at some time in the year or the pasture will become impoverished.

Chain harrowing when the pasture is dry in the early spring and before housed sheep are turned out with their lambs, will remove dead material from the turf and scatter droppings. It will also encourage new growth in the grass.

The pasture can be improved by the clearance of any unpalatable weeds, nettles, thistles, docks, etc. If the acreage is small, the docks can be dug out by hand and the nettles and thistles, if cut regularly through the growing period, will eventually succumb. The sheep will often eat the cut material once it has wilted. Ragwort can pose a problem. The sheep will graze it when it is a rosette of leaves in the early spring without any ill-effects, but later in the season if allowed to grow to the flowering stage it is poisonous to sheep. If it gets included in hay or is cut and left to wilt and then eaten, the accumulation of poison will eventually kill the animal.

Regular mowing to contain the surplus grass even while the sheep are still grazing will improve the pasture. Once the grass gets to the flowering stage, it does not produce much more leaf, which is the nutritious part of the plant. Regular mowing will prevent the grass from flowering or running to seed, thus promoting further growth of leaf.

Regular mowing will also prevent weeds from seeding and increasing their population in the sward. More of the sheep droppings will be exposed to sunlight which will lead to a lower rate of infestation by internal parasites because of the effect it has on the eggs of the roundworms.

If it is possible to subdivide the pasture more involved procedures can be undertaken. The old turf can be treated with a herbicide to kill it off and a rotovator used to cultivate the surface before sowing new grass and clover seed. When choosing new grass seed, select leafy strains of ryegrass for the main part of the mixture and add white clover and deep-rooting herbs. White clover with its ability to fix nitrogen from the air, to the benefit of the accompanying grass, is also high in energy, protein, minerals and vitamins. In addition to giving variety to the mixture, the herbs chicory, burnet and yarrow will help by bringing up minerals from below the level to which the roots of the grass penetrate.

Any quantity of surplus grass can be fenced off using temporary electric fencing and be made into hay. In view of the machinery involved, this is a job for a local contractor. Cut the grass when it is at the early flowering stage and if possible get it dry and baled without allowing any rain on it, then stack it under cover. The regrowth, or aftermath, provides valuable feed for newly weaned lambs as it is clean and the risk of parasitic infection is much less, due to the break in the life cycle of the parasites when the hay crop is taken off. It can be advantageous if cattle are available to assist in controlling the surplus grass and keeping the sward short. This also helps to control parasites.

Appendices

Appendices

Some Plants poisonous to sheep

Most poisonous plants are avoided by sheep unless grazing is very sparse as in times of drought or during spells of severe weather, especially snowstorms. The main danger comes when they are cut, wilted and made into hay, often unnoticed, and are then readily eaten by the sheep.

Yew. Probably the plant causing most problems for the small flock owner is the yew. If only a small quantity is eaten the animal will die. This applies to the living shrub or tree, and also to any hedge trimmings which may inadvertently be dumped where the sheep have access to them.

Bracken. This is poisonous to stock but to a much lesser extent than yew, and will normally be eaten only when grazing is in short supply or when it is made into hay or used as bedding. Sheep affected by bracken poisoning become blind.

Equisetum or horsetail. Not usually a problem unless cut, dried and made into hay. If it is then eaten, it is poisonous and there is no antidote. The sheep dies.

Laburnum. Sheep seem to be less affected by eating this tree than some other types of livestock. All parts of the tree are poisonous and will cause death if consumed in quantity.

Acorns. These are sometimes eaten in quantity by sheep who inexplicably develop a craving for them. They are more poisonous when green and unripe. Affected animals suffer from constipation, which is then quickly followed by diarrhoea. They should be moved away from the source as quickly as possible.

Azaleas and rhododendrons. These plants often 'escape' into boundary fences from gardens and woodlands and can cause considerable damage to the nervous system if eaten. As with yew, the clippings from gardens are as toxic when wilted as when they are green. The shrub should either be removed completely or fenced off out of reach of the sheep, as ewes seeking extra nutrition in the weeks just prior to lambing will readily eat it, having avoided it completely for months before.

Ragwort. This should be pulled out and burned before it reaches the flowering stage (see Chapter Twelve). The toxin accumulates in sheep if they are given hay containing the dried plant.

Sheep Names and Terms

In different parts of the country, different names are given to the various ages of sheep and this can be confusing for the new flock owner. Some names are in common usage, however, and lamb is the universal name given to the newly born. The lambs can be either ram lambs or ewe lambs and they carry this name through the summer even after they are weaned. When the lamb wool breaks to form locks, the wool then forms a tapering point on each lock, similar to the tag on an old-fashioned shoe lace, and tag, or more commonly teg, is the word used to describe the age of sheep. The term hogg or hogget is also used in some parts of the country.

A ewe and her lamb are spoken of as a couple and where there are twins as a double couple.

Chilver is the name given to females in south-west Engliand, and gimmer is commonly used in Scotland and the north of England to describe female sheep after their first shearing. Theave is also a name used in parts of England for once shorn ewes, while in all areas shearling refers to both males and females between their first and second shearings. Subsequently they can be known as two-shear, three-shear or four-shear rams or ewes.

Sometimes the number of permanent incisor teeth present is used to describe the age of the sheep, and a shearling becomes a two-tooth, a two-shear a four-tooth, a three-shear is a six-tooth and a four-shear is known as full-mouthed.

In hill flocks a substantial income is derived from selling cast ewes. These are ewes which have reached maturity and still have sound teeth and udders, and which can be replaced by the annual intake of shearling ewes bred in the flock. The cast ewes are sold to lowland farmers for crossbreeding where they do not have to withstand the rigours of the climate often experienced by hill sheep. They are sometimes described as draft ewes in other parts of the country. A broken-mouthed ewe or crone is one which has lost some incisor teeth through age but which may still be capable of breeding and rearing lambs, provided that the udder is sound.
A ewe which does not breed when given the opportunity to do so is called either barren, guest or eild.

A cull ewe is one which is not retained for breeding for any reason – chronic ill-health, poor conformation, or as a non-breeder – and which is sold with no guarantee as to its fitness for future breeding.

A wether is a castrated male sheep, and a rig is a male sheep which has either one or both testicles undescended.

Some Organisations Serving the Sheep Industry

The National Sheep Association (NSA), The Sheep Centre
Malvern, Worcs, WR13 6PH. 01684 892661

Originally called the National Sheepbreeders Association, it became the National Sheep Association in 1969. It is involved in all aspects of the sheep industry and is financed entirely by members with an interest in sheep and by commercial concerns with a direct interest in the industry. The NSA promotes the industry to those involved in agriculture at home and abroad, and ensures that the appropriate authorities understand the views of the British sheep farmer.

The Rare Breeds Survival Trust, National Agricultural Centre
Kenilworth, Warks, CV8 2LG. 01203 696551

Organic Sheep Society, Worcester College of Agriculture
Hindlip, Worcs, WR3 8SS. 01905 513103

British Wool Marketing Board, Oak Mills, Station Road, Clayton,
Bradford, BD14 6JD. 01274 882091

Meat and Livestock Commission, PO Box 44, Winterhill House
Milton Keynes, Bucks, MK6 1AX. 01908 677577

Advice on the design of sheep housing may be obtained from ADAS
at the local offices of DEFRA.

The Shepherds Kit

Certain essentials of kit and equipment are necessary to enable the
beginner to cope adequately with specific tasks which periodically
require attention. A suggested list includes:

- Foot trimming shears for keeping the sheep's feet in good shape and assisting with footrot prevention.
- A sharp pocket knife for paring away under-run horn if infected with footrot.
- Disposable syringes with spare needles for vaccinating and administering antibiotics or for injecting calcium borogluconate to counter calcium and magnesium deficiencies.
- A bottle of calcium borogluconate.
- Halters for holding and restraining a sheep when necessary.
- Dagging shears, 15cm bladed shears for removing wool soiled with faeces and urine
- Sharpening stone.
- Combined insecticide and antiseptic, available in cream or powder form, for treating maggots, shear cuts and external wounds.
- Antibiotic aerosol spray for treating wounds,

available from your vet.
- Mild disinfectant, soap and towel.
- Disposable plastic gloves, essential when dealing with sheep infected with the orf virus.
- Fleece branding irons for use with marking fluid.
- Paint aerosols, crayons and tins of marking fluid.
- Drenching equipment for administering anthelmintics.
- A kneeling pad for use in inclement weather.
- Your veterinary surgeon's telephone number.

These items should be kept ready for use in a clean condition in a suitable container.

Sheep Dairying

Sheep dairying is another option which may be considered by the beginner. The Friesland and the British Milksheep are probably the two main breeds used for milk production, although crosses using these breeds as sires can also give useful yields. A yield of around 250 litres per ewe per year is necessary for a viable enterprise, and further value can be added by converting the milk into yoghurt, cheese or ice-cream.

Milk production can be a costly business to set up as, in addition to the cost of the ewes and rams, buildings will be needed to house the equipment and they must be of a high standard. The same standards of hygiene apply as in milk production from cattle. Sheep milk comes under the Food Act (1990) and all areas require inspection by an ADAS officer. Local Environmental Health Officers will wish to inspect areas used for processing, and advice should be sought before starting on such an enterprise.

Sheep Societies

Balwen Welsh Mountain Sheep Society, Ty-Deri, Llanethrine, Abergavenny, Gwent, NP7 8PY. Tel: 01873 821224. Contact: Mr Chris Lewis

Beltex Sheep Society, Lawns Farm, Orrell, Wigan, Lancashire WN5 8UH
Tel: 01695 627626, Fax: 01695 627626. Web: www.shorthorn.co.uk

Blackface Sheep Breeders Association, Brae View, Drumharvie, Crieff, PH7 3PG. Tel: 01764 683746, Fax: 01764 683746
Web: www.scottish-blackface.co.uk. Contact: Mrs A Mcfadzean

Bluefaced Leicester Sheep Breeders Association, Regent House, Bank Street, Annan DG12 6AA. Tel: 01461 206900, Fax: 01461 206903
Web: www.blueleicester.co.uk. Contact: Mrs F Sloan

Brecknock Hill Cheviot Sheep Society, 13 Lion Street, Brecon, Powys LD3 7HY. Tel: 01874 622488. Contact: Mr Peter Francis,

British Alpine Breed Society, The Old Tanyard, Pound Pill, Corsham, Wiltshire SN13 9HT. Tel: 01249 716350. Contact: Mrs S C Head

British Berrichon Du Cher Sheep Society, Woodston Manor, Lindridge, Tenbury Wells, Worcs WR15 8JG. Tel: 01584 881657
Web: www.berrichonsociety.com. Contact: Emma Hillhouse

British Bleu Du Maine Sheep Society, Fayre Oaks, Trostrey, Usk, Monmouthshire NP15 1LA. Tel: 01291 673816, Fax: 01291 673889
Web: www.bleudumaine.co.uk, Contact: Ms Jane Smith

British Charollais Sheep Society, Youngmans Road, Wymondham, Norfolk, NR18 0RR. Tel: 01953 603334, Fax: 01953 607626
Contact: Mrs Carroll Baker

British Friesland Sheep Society, Weir Park Farm, Waterwell Lane, Christow, Exeter, Devon EX6 7PB. Tel: 01647 252549. Contact: Mrs L Baber

British Gotland Sheep Society, Greendale, East Allington, Totnes, Devon TQ9 7R. Tel: 01548 521388. Contact: Mrs Mary Mylne

British Icelandic Sheep Breeders Group, Ramsden Heath Farm, Witney Road, Ramsden, Chipping Norton, Oxfordshire OX7 3AS
Tel: 01993 868704. Contact: Mrs Mary Castell,

British Milksheep Society, St Kenelms, Broad Lane, Tamworth-In-Arden, Solihull, West Midlands B94 5HX. Tel: 01564 742398. Contact: Mr William Hopkins,

British Rouge De L'ouest Sheep Society Ltd., Bowling Green Farm, Yarnscombe, Barnstaple, North Devon EX31 3LW. Tel: 0845 600 1503.
Web: www.rouge-society.co.uk. Contact: Mrs Debbie Siggs

British Texel Sheep Society, 4th Street, National Agricultural Centre, Stoneleigh Park, Kenilworth Warwickshire CV8 2LG. Tel: 02476 696629,
Fax: 02476 696472. Web: www.texel.co.uk. Contact: Mr K Campbell

Cambridge Sheep Society, Pharm House, Neston Road, Willaston In Wirral, Neston,,Cheshire CH6 2TL. Tel: 0151 794 6103. Contact: Mr A Davies,

Castlemilk Moorit Sheep Society, Creacombemoor Cottage, Rackenford, Tiverton, Devon EX16 8EN. Tel: 01884 881222. Contact: Mr J Sanders,

Cheviot Sheep Society, Holm Cottage, Langholm, Dunfries & Galloway DG13 0JP.
Tel: 01387 380222. Web: www.cheviotsheep.org. Contact: Ms Isobel J Mcvittie

Clun Forest Sheep Breeders Ltd., The Livestock Market, The Ox Pasture, Overton Road, Ludlow Shropshire SY8 4AH. Tel: 01584 872251. Contact: Mr D Uffold

Colbred Sheep Society, Crickley Barrow, Northleach, Cheltenham, Gloucestershire GL54 3QA. Tel: 01451 60330. Contact: Mr A O Colburn

Pentervin Farm, Minsterley, Shropshire SY5 0HD
Tel: 01743 891347. Contact: Mr David Littlehales

Cotswold Sheep Society, The Oaks, Kenley, Nr Shrewsbury Shropshire SY5 6NR.
Tel: 01694 771899, Fax: 01694 771899. Web: www.cotswoldsheep.org

Dalesbred Sheep Breeders Association, Gib Hey Cottage, Chipping, Nr Preston, Lancashire PR3 2WU. Tel: 01995 61570. Contact: Mr J Whitaker,

Derbyshire Gritstone Sheep Breeders Society, 5 Bridge Close, Waterfoot, Rossendale, Lancashire BB4 9SN. Tel: 01706 228520. Contact: Mrs S Coppack,

Devon And Cornwall Longwool Flockbook Association, Peckham View, Kentisbeare, Cullompton, Devon EX15 2EY. Tel: 01884 266201. Contact: Mr M Britton

Dorset Horn & Dorset Poll Sheep Breeders Association, Agriculture House, Acland Road, Dorchester, Dorset DT1 1EF. Tel: 01305 262176,
Fax: 01305 262126. Web: www.dorsetsheep.org. Contact: Mrs Margarite Crowley

Eppynt Hill & Beulah Speckled Face Sheep Society, C/O Brightwells, Market Office, Smithfield Road, Builth Wells, Powys LD2 3AN
Tel: 01982 553614. Contact: Mr D Jones

Sheep Societies

Est A Laine Merino Sheep Society, The Merino Centre, Wymondham, Norfolk NR18 0RR. Tel: 01953 607860. Contact: Mrs C Barber

Exmoor Horn Sheep Breeders' Society, Holton & Thomasthe Elm Office, Bishops Tawton, Barnstaple, Devon EX32 0EJ
Tel: 01271 326900, Fax: 01271 326692. Contact: Mrs Yvonne Webber

Galway Sheep Breeders Society, Hill Croft, Ingoe, Matfen, Newcastle Upon Tyne NE20 0SJ. Tel: 01661 886408. Web: www.sheep.ukf.net. Contact: Mr Alan Cheese

Greyface Dartmoor Sheep Breeders Association, The Old Rectory, Clannaborough, Crediton, Devon EX17 6DA. Tel: 01363 85205

Hampshire Down Sheep Breeders Association, Rickyard Cottage, Denner Hill, Great Messenden, Buckinghamshire HP16 0HZ.
Tel: 01494 488388. Contact: Mr R Daviis

Hebridean Sheep Society, Knox Mill, Knox Mill Lane, Harrogate, N Yorkshire HG3 2AE. Tel: 0705 003 9598. Web: www.hebrideansheep.org.uk. Contact: Mr E Medway

Herdwick Sheep Breeders Association, The Old Stables, Redhills, Penrith, Cumbria CA11 0DT. Tel: 01768 869533, Fax: 01768 242134. Contact: Mr G Brown

Hill Radnor Flock Book Society, 16 Ship Street, Brecon, Powys LD3 9AD
Tel: 01874 623200

Ile De France Sheep Society, Kingdons Farm, Gummow Shop, Newquay, Cornwall TR8 4PP. Tel: 01872 510636

Jacob Sheep Society, Foxholes Farm, Hanbury, Burton-On-Trent, Staffordshire DE13 8QT. Tel: 01283 820487, Fax: 01283 820487
Web: www.jacobsheep.org.uk. Contact: Ms Annabel Briggs

Kerry Hill Flock Book Society, Brynteg, Penygarnedd, Llanrhaeadr-Y-Mochnant, Oswestery, Shropshire SY10 0AW. Tel: 01691 860336. Contact: Ms Gill Napper

Leicester Longwool Sheep Breeders Association, The Showground, Kelleythorpe, Driffield East Yorkshire YO25 9DN. Tel: 01377 257494. Contact: Mrs Ilnes

Lincoln Longwool Sheep Breeders Association, Lincolnshire Showground, Grange-De-Lings, Lincoln, Lincolnshire LN2 2NA. Tel: 01522 511395. Contact: Mr J Skehel

Llamvenog Sheep Society, Nantgwyn, Llanfair Road, Lampeter, Ceredigion SA48 8JY.
Tel: 01570 423135. Web: www.llanwenog-sheep.co.uk. Contact: Miss Meinir Green

Lleyn Sheep Society, Gwyndy, Bryncroes, Sarn, Pwllheli, Gwynedd LL53 8FT
Tel: 01758 730366, 01758 790578. Contact: Ms Gwenda Roberts

Lonk Sheep Breeders Association, 51 Glen View, Burnley, Lancashire BB11 2QW. Tel:
01282 433017. Contact: Mrs J Shorrock

Manx Loghtan Sheep Breeders Group, Dairy Barn, North Houghton, Stockbridge,
Hampshire SO20 6LF. Tel: 01264 810274. Contact: Mrs J Gotting

Marsham Sheep Breeders Association, Oak Bank, Bentham, Lancaster, Lancashire
LA2 7DW. Tel: 01524 561606. Contact: Mrs V J Lawson

Norfolk Horn Breeders Group, Park Farm, The Old Rectory, Anmer, Kings Lynn,
Norfolk PE31 6RN. Tel: 01485 600824. Contact: Mrs K E Long

North County Cheviot Sheep Society, 16 St Vincent Road, Tain, Ross-Shire IV19 1JR.
Tel: 01862 894014. Web: www.nc.cheviot.co.uk. Contact: Mr William Morrison

North Of England Mule Sheep Association, Eslaforde, Weir View, Frosterley, Bishops
Auckland, County Durham DL13 2RB. Tel: 01388 527411, Fax: 01388 526728.
Website: www.nemsa.co.uk. Contact: Mrs D Bell,

Oxford Down Sheep Breeders Association, Bishops Gorse, Lighthorne,
Warwickshire CV35 60B. Tel: 01926 651273. Contact: Mr John Brigg

Portland Sheep Breeders Group, Hogchester Farm, Wooton Fitzpaine, Nr
Charmouth, Dorset DT6 6BY. Tel: 01297 561072. Contact: Mrs M Jones

Romney Sheep Breeders Society, 2 Woodland Close, West Malling, Kent ME19 6RR.
Tel: 01732 854637. Contact: Mr Alan West

Rough Fell Sheep Breeders Association, Weasdale Farm, Newbiggin In Lune, Kirby
Stephen, Cumbria CA17 4LY. Tel: 01539 623238. Contact: Mrs P Tyson

Roussin Sheep Society, Lentra, The Park, Thornhill, Dumfriesshire DG3 5JT
Tel: 01848 331640. Contact: Contact: Mr A Wright

Ryeland Flock Book Society Ltd, Holly Cottage, Redmarley D'abitot,
Gloucestershire GL19 3NB. Tel: 01531 650400. Contact: Mrs Anne M Jones

Scottish Mule Association, Station House, Collessie, Cupar, Fife KY15 7RQ
Tel: 01337 810230. Contact: Mrs S Jackson

Shetland Sheep Breeders Group, Acre Cottage, Horsebridge, King's Somborne,
Hampshire SO20 6PT. Tel: 01794 388057. Contact: Mr Jim Johnson

Shetland-Cheviot Marketing Society, Fairview, Vidlin, Shetland ZE2 9GB
Tel: 01806 577227. Contact: Mr J Johnson

Shropshire Sheep Breeders Association, Stable Views, Alderton, Nr Montford
Bridge, Shrewsbury, Shropshire SY4 1AW. Tel: 01743 741689, Fax: 01743 741113.
Contact: Mrs Pipppa Geddes,

South Wales Mountain Sheep Society, 40 Rhys Road, Blackwood, Caerphilly County
Borough, Gwent NP12 3UR. Tel: 01443 839234. Contact: Mr G Davies

Suffolk Sheep Society, The Sheep Centre, Malvern, Worcestershire WR13 6PH. Tel:
01684 893366, Fax: 01684 893390

Swaledale Sheep Breeders Association, The Shooting Lodge, High Shipley, Eggleston,
Barnard Castle, County Durham DL12 0NP
Tel: 01833 650516. Contact: Mr John Stephenson

Teeswater Sheep Breeders Association Ltd, Wodencroft, Cotherstone, Barnard
Castle, County Durham DL12 9UQ. Tel: 01833 650032. Contact: Mrs M Braithwaite

The Badger Face Welsh Mountain Sheep Society, Bryn Hyfryd, Ty Maur Lane,
Llanegfan, Menai Bridge, Sir Fon LL59 5TR
Tel: 01248 713183. Contact: Mrs Madeleine Pritchard

The British Inra 401 Sheep Society. Sheldon Grange, Dunkeswell, Honiton, Devon
EX14 0RW. Tel: 01823 680565. Contact: Mr G F Burrough

The Devon Closewool Sheep Breeders Society, Holton & Thomas, The Elm Office,
Bishops Tawton, Barnstaple, Devon EX32 0EJ
Tel: 01271 326900, Fax: 01271 326692. Contact: Mr Ron Smith

The Society Of Border Leicester Sheep Breeders, Greenend, St Boswells, Melrose,
Borders TD6 9ES. Tel: 01835 824207, 01835 824207
Web: www.borderleicesters.co.uk. Contact: Ms Nesta D Todd

The Southdown Sheep Society, Southdown Lodge, 300 Cople Road, Cardington,
Bedfordshire MK44 3SH. Tel: 01234 838807.
Web: www.southdownsheepsociety.com.uk
Contact: Mr Clive Pritchard Ba, Llb (Hons) Llm (Wales)

Vendeen Sheep Society Ltd, 20 Brookfield Drive, Wolvey, Hinckley, Leicestershire
LE10 3TL. Tel: 01455 220456

Welsh Hill Speckled Face Sheep Society, Morris Marshall & Poole, Bank House,
Great Oak Street, Llanudloes, Powys SY18 6BW
Tel: 01686 440279. Contact: Mr R Griffiths

Welsh Mountain Sheep Society - Hill Flock Section, P O Box 8, 'Gorseland', North Road, Aberystwyth, Ceredigion SY23 2HE
Tel: 01970 636688. Contact: Mr W G M Jones

Welsh Mountain Sheep Society - Pedigree Section, 52 Ffordd Celyn, Denbigh, Clwyd LL16 5UU. Tel: 01745 814289
Contact: Mr M Voyle Erw Myrddin

Wensleydale Longwool Sheep Breeders Association, Whichway Cottage, 6 Coventry Road, Princethorpe, Nr Rugby Warwickshire CV23 9QF
Tel: 01926 633439. Contact: Dr D L Clouder
White Face Dartmoor Sheep Group, 13 West Street, Ashburton, Devon TQ13 7DZ. Tel: 01364 652304, 01364 652695. Contact: Mr G T Chambers

White Faced Woodland Breeders Group, 2 Biddlesdon, Brackley, Northants NN13 5TR. Tel: 01280 850677. Contact: Mrs C Muddiman

Wiltshire Horn Sheep Society, 7 High Street, Kislingbury, Northampton, Northants NN7 4AQ. Tel: 01604 833548. Contact: Ms Ann Elliott

Zwatbles Sheep Association, Manor Field, Frome St Quinton, Dorchester, Dorset DT2 0HF. Tel: 01935 83395. Contact: Mrs Penny Aikenhead

About the Authors
Jane Upton
Having trained in art and design and worked in London for many years, Jane Upton moved to the country. She works as a freelance artist and photographer, specialising principally in medical illustration. Her interest in sheep started when she was given a single ewe as a present and there followed several 'surprise' lambs. With the help of other local sheep keepers and various publications, but principally with practical guidance and encouragement from Dennis Soden, she now has a healthy, established flock of Suffolks. Her new book, The Shepherd's Companion, is due to be published by Farming Books and Videos Ltd. in 2008.

Dennis Soden
Dennis Soden had a lifetime of interest in sheep, which began with work with a leading show shepherd following his military service. His varied experience throughout Britain includes work with a large commercial flock and a stint as Field Officer with the Sheep Development Association. He also visited sheep properties in Australia and for eight years was a technician at Merrist Wood Agricultural College. When he retired he continued to be active with small-scale sheep keepers who suggested that he write this book with Jane Upton ensuring his knowledge of shepherding and handling sheep be passed on to a new generation of sheepkeepers. Dennis died in 2005.

Farming Books and Videos Ltd.

PO Box 536, Preston, PR2 9ZY.
Telephone 01772 652693
www.farmingbooksandvideos.com

Farming Books and Videos Ltd. is a family run, independant publishing company specialising in titles for the farmer, smallholder and country-dweller.

Other titles include:

A Cut Above the Rest DVD *covering the butchering of lamb, pork and poultry*
The Sausage Book by Paul Peacock.
Traditional Cattle Breeds by Peter King
The Shepherd's Pup DVD
Talking Sheepdogs by Derek Scrimgeour
A Guide to Traditional Pig Keeping by Carol Harris
Not Just for Christmas. *The Complete guide to Raising Turkeys* by Janice Houghton-Wallace
The Smoking and Curing Book by Paul Peacock
Jack Hargreaves - A Portrait by Paul Peacock
The Cheesemaking Book by Paul Peacock
Nature's Harvest by Paul Peacock
The Secret Life of Cows by Rosamund Young
The Polytunnel Companion by Jayne Neville
The Shepherd's Companion by Jane Upton *is being published by Farming Books and Videos Ltd in* Farming Books and Videos Ltd.,

Index

Index